Critical Existential-Analytic Psychotherapy

This book is an introduction to critical existential-analytic psychotherapy. It has been written as a response to what is considered to be a crisis point in what is currently taken as psychotherapeutic knowledge. A focus point is the relentless move in psychotherapy and psychotherapy trainings towards evidence-based practice. It is suggested that such developments can be usefully challenged if we are to consider:

- Can starting with theory be a form of violence?
- Should a primacy be given to practice?
- Does a reliance on empirical research mean we start from the wrong place?

From a critical existential-analytic psychotherapeutic perspective, the answer to all three of these questions is 'yes'. This perspective, therefore, is fundamentally different from what psychological therapists are increasingly purporting to do, and further challenges other current notions from diagnosis and treatment to dominant discourses in psychology.

The aim of this book is to consider some ways in which the psychological therapies might be able to move away from the crisis mainly caused by what is currently wrongly being understood in terms of 'evidence-based practice' as the nature of psychotherapeutic knowledge. Instead, it is proposed that primacy be given to: practice, considering theories having implications rather than applications, and privileging thoughtfulness with notions of research being seen more as cultural practices.

This book is based on a special issue of the *European Journal of Psychotherapy & Counselling*.

Del Loewenthal is Emeritus Professor of Psychotherapy and Counselling at the University of Roehampton and is Chair of the Southern Association for Psychotherapy and Counselling (SAFPAC), London, UK. He is an existential-analytic psychotherapist and chartered psychologist, with a particular interest in phenomenology. His books include *Existential Psychotherapy and Counselling after Postmodernism* (Routledge, 2017). www.delloewenthal.com; www.safpac.co.uk.

Critical Existential-Analytic Psychotherapy
Some Implications for Practices, Theories and Research

Edited by
Del Loewenthal

LONDON AND NEW YORK

First published 2021
by Routledge
2 Park Square, Milton Park, Abingdon, Oxon OX14 4RN

and by Routledge
52 Vanderbilt Avenue, New York, NY 10017

Routledge is an imprint of the Taylor & Francis Group, an informa business

Introduction, Chapters 1–9 © 2021 Taylor & Francis
Chapter 10 © 2011 Del Loewenthal

All rights reserved. No part of this book may be reprinted or reproduced or utilised in any form or by any electronic, mechanical, or other means, now known or hereafter invented, including photocopying and recording, or in any information storage or retrieval system, without permission in writing from the publishers.

Trademark notice: Product or corporate names may be trademarks or registered trademarks, and are used only for identification and explanation without intent to infringe.

British Library Cataloguing in Publication Data
A catalogue record for this book is available from the British Library

ISBN: 978-0-367-69054-0 (hbk)
ISBN: 978-1-003-14027-6 (ebk)

Typeset in Minion Pro
by Newgen Publishing UK

Publisher's Note
The publisher accepts responsibility for any inconsistencies that may have arisen during the conversion of this book from journal articles to book chapters, namely the inclusion of journal terminology.

Disclaimer
Every effort has been made to contact copyright holders for their permission to reprint material in this book. The publishers would be grateful to hear from any copyright holder who is not here acknowledged and will undertake to rectify any errors or omissions in future editions of this book.

Contents

Citation Information   vii
Notes on Contributors   ix

Introduction   1
Del Loewenthal

1 Looking like a foreigner: Foreignness, conformity and compliance in psychoanalysis   10
Onel Brooks

2 Language as Gesture in Merleau-Ponty: Some implications for method in therapeutic practice and research   29
Julia Cayne

3 The private life of meaning – some implications for psychotherapy and psychotherapeutic research   42
Tony McSherry, Del Loewenthal and Julia Cayne

4 Finding my voice: Telling stories with heuristic self-search inquiry   57
Elizabeth Nicholl, Del Loewenthal and James Davies

5 'When working in a youth service, how do therapists experience humour with their clients?'   74
Patricia Talens

6 What gets in the way of working with clients who have been sexually abused? Heuristic inquiry   88
Iana Trichkova, Del Loewenthal, Betty Bertrand and Catherine Altson

7 Maculate conceptions   103
Manu Bazzano

8 The pictures you paint in the stories you tell, a response *Laura Chernaik*	117
9 Reflections on the tensions between openness and method in experientially oriented research and psychotherapy *Steen Halling*	130
10 On the very idea of post-existentialism *Del Loewenthal*	143
Index	152

Citation Information

The following chapters, except Chapter 10, were originally published in the *European Journal of Psychotherapy & Counselling*, volume 22, issue 1–2 (2020). When citing this material, please use the original page numbering for each article, as follows:

Chapter 1
Looking like a foreigner: Foreignness, conformity and compliance in psychoanalysis
Onel Brooks
European Journal of Psychotherapy & Counselling, volume 22, issue 1–2 (2020), pp. 9–29

Chapter 2
Language as Gesture in Merleau-Ponty: Some implications for method in therapeutic practice and research
Julia Cayne
European Journal of Psychotherapy & Counselling, volume 22, issue 1–2 (2020), pp. 30–44

Chapter 3
The private life of meaning – some implications for psychotherapy and psychotherapeutic research
Tony McSherry, Del Loewenthal and Julia Cayne
European Journal of Psychotherapy & Counselling, volume 22, issue 1–2 (2020), pp. 45–60

Chapter 4
Finding my voice: Telling stories with heuristic self-search inquiry
Elizabeth Nicholl, Del Loewenthal and James Davies
European Journal of Psychotherapy & Counselling, volume 22, issue 1–2 (2020), pp. 61–79

Chapter 5
'When working in a youth service, how do therapists experience humour with their clients?'
Patricia Talens
European Journal of Psychotherapy & Counselling, volume 22, issue 1–2 (2020), pp. 80–96

Chapter 6
What gets in the way of working with clients who have been sexually abused? Heuristic inquiry
Iana Trichkova, Del Loewenthal, Betty Bertrand and Catherine Altson
European Journal of Psychotherapy & Counselling, volume 22, issue 1–2 (2020), pp. 97–113

Chapter 7
Maculate conceptions
Manu Bazzano
European Journal of Psychotherapy & Counselling, volume 22, issue 1–2 (2020), pp. 114–128

Chapter 8
The pictures you paint in the stories you tell, a response
Laura Chernaik
European Journal of Psychotherapy & Counselling, volume 22, issue 1–2 (2020), pp. 129–142

Chapter 9
Reflections on the tensions between openness and method in experientially oriented research and psychotherapy
Steen Halling
European Journal of Psychotherapy & Counselling, volume 22, issue 1–2 (2020), pp. 143–156

Chapter 10
Loewenthal, D. (2011). On the very idea of post-existentialism. In D. Loewenthal, *Post Existentialism and the Psychological Therapies: Towards a Therapy without Foundations*. London: Karnac (pp. 1–12).

For any permission-related enquiries please visit:
www.tandfonline.com/page/help/permissions

Notes on Contributors

Catherine Altson is a counsellor and lecturer, currently working in private practice in Kingston-upon-Thames, UK, and as Lecturer in Humanistic-Existential Counselling at Guildford College, London, UK. Her main research interests revolve around the ways in which counsellors' and psychotherapists' lives are influenced by their clinical practice. Catherine is an associate member of the Southern Association for Psychotherapy and Counselling (SAFPAC), London, UK, and previously lectured in the Research Centre for Therapeutic Education, University of Roehampton, London, UK.

Manu Bazzano is a writer, editor, psychotherapist and supervisor in private practice. He is an internationally recognised lecturer and workshop facilitator. His books include: *Nietzsche and Psychotherapy* (2019); *Re-Visioning Person-Centred Therapy* (Ed., 2018); *Zen and Therapy: Heretical Perspectives* (2017); *After Mindfulness* (Ed., 2014); and *Spectre of the Stranger: Towards a Phenomenology of Hospitality* (2012).

Betty Bertrand is a French psychotherapist in private practice in London and the South of France. Her experience covers a wide range of institutions, including prisons. Her current work focuses on the psychological implications of expatriation. Betty practises mainly online with expats from various nationalities who live across the world. Betty is an associate member of the Southern Association for Psychotherapy and Counselling (SAFPAC), London, UK, and was previously a lecturer in the Research Centre for Therapeutic Education, University of Roehampton, London, UK.

Onel Brooks is particularly interested in philosophy and psychoanalysis. He is a core member of the Southern Association for Psychotherapy and Counselling (SAFPAC) teaching team (www.safpac.co.uk) and Senior Lecturer in Psychotherapy, Counselling and Counselling Psychology in the Psychology Department, Roehampton University, London, UK. He is BACP (British Association for Counselling and Psychotherapy) accredited and UKCP (UK Council for Psychotherapy) registered as a psychoanalytic psychotherapist and as an existential-analytic psychotherapist. He worked for many years with adolescents and adults, in therapeutic communities, the NHS and in voluntary organisations, as well as in universities. He also contributes to the teaching at the Philadelphia Association, London, UK.

Julia Cayne is Visiting Lecturer in the Research Centre for Therapeutic Education at the University of Roehampton, London, UK, and is an existential-analytic psychotherapist, with a private practice in Salisbury, UK. She completed her PhD thesis on learning about the unknown and developing a methodology to explore such phenomena. She is involved with the Southern Association for Psychotherapy and Counselling (SAFPAC), London, UK, which provides training in critical existential-analytic psychotherapy, as well as supervising doctoral research through the University of Roehampton.

Laura Chernaik is a psychoanalyst in private practice and is a member of the Site for Contemporary Psychoanalysis, London, UK. Her publications include *Social and Virtual Space* (Fairleigh Dickinson Press, 2005) and *New Hope*, a novel (Kindle, 2016).

James Davies is Reader in Medical Anthropology and Mental Health at the University of Roehampton, London, UK.

Steen Halling is Licensed Psychologist and Professor Emeritus of Psychology at Seattle University, USA, where he has taught in the MA programme in existential-phenomenological psychology as well as in the undergraduate programme since 1976. His research and publications have focused on topics such as the psychology of forgiveness, the phenomenological study of psychopathology, the psychology of hopelessness, envy, interpersonal relations, and qualitative research methods.

Del Loewenthal is Emeritus Professor of Psychotherapy and Counselling at the University of Roehampton, London, UK, and is Chair of the Southern Association for Psychotherapy and Counselling (SAFPAC), London, UK. He is an existential-analytic psychotherapist and chartered psychologist, with a particular interest in phenomenology. His books include *Existential Psychotherapy and Counselling after Postmodernism* (Routledge, 2017). www.delloewenthal.com; www.safpac.co.uk.

Tony McSherry is an existential-analytical psychotherapist working in the NHS and private practice in Liverpool, UK. He recently completed his PhD on the therapeutic in mental health nursing at the University of Roehampton, London, UK.

Elizabeth Nicholl is an existential-analytic psychotherapist and a member of the Southern Association for Psychotherapy and Counselling (SAFPAC),

London, UK. She recently gained a PhD in psychotherapy at the University of Roehampton, London, UK. She has a private practice in Dorset and Wiltshire, UK.

Patricia Talens, MUPCA, is a practicing psychotherapeutic counsellor based in London. She graduated with a BA (Hons) in criminology and applied psychology before spending six years working in forensic mental health. She completed her MSc in counselling and psychotherapy with a special interest in the role of therapeutic research and practice.

Iana Trichkova completed her MSc in counselling and psychotherapy at the University of Roehampton, London, UK, and is currently undertaking PhD research focused on psychotherapists' sexuality. She is Visiting Lecturer at Regent's University London, UK. She works as a psychotherapist in private practice and in a forensic setting. She is a registered member of the British Association for Counselling and Psychotherapy (BACP) and is a member of the Universities Psychotherapy and Counselling Association (UPCA).

Introduction

Del Loewenthal

Has a crisis point been reached in what is currently viewed as psychotherapeutic knowledge? There are, for example, an ever-increasing number of continuous professional development (CPD) courses offering to help therapists with everything from abandonment to maternal deprivation. Could such CPD, which might be typical of psychotherapy trainings that assume some form of diagnosis and treatment, be usefully challenged if we were to consider that:

- to start with theory can be a form of violence?
- primacy should be given to practice?
- reliance on empirical research means we start from the wrong place?

From a critical existential-analytic psychotherapeutic perspective, which is an evolution of what I have otherwise called 'post-existentialism', the answer to all three of these assertions is 'yes'. This perspective therefore may be fundamentally different from what psychological therapists are increasingly purporting to do, though there may be less divergence, in albeit a decreasing number of cases, in what is *actually* their practice. (It may also be that this newly created generic term of 'psychological therapist' is as different to the various 'therapists' it collectively now represents as, it will shortly be considered, 'phenomenological research' is from 'phenomenology'.)

This fundamentally different approach is also explored in Loewenthal (2020a), where the aspects listed in Table 1 are considered further. However, rather than comparing existentialism with post-existentialism, the table compares evidence-based psychotherapies with critical existential-analytic psychotherapies ('post-existential' being the forerunner of 'critical existential-analytic').

Table 1 indicates the fundamental different potential implications of the approach advocated here, which underly 'critical existential-analytic psychotherapies'. Such approaches can be seen as an attempt to be clearer with another person about his or her meanings and experiences. However, doesn't the therapist then have to work with each client's unique, though culturally influenced, language and interpretation? Further, whilst for the therapist there are such questions as those of judgement (and timing), isn't psychotherapy

Table 1 A comparison of aspects of evidence-based psychotherapies with critical existential-analytic psychotherapies

	Evidence-based practice psychotherapies	Critical existential-analytic psychotherapies
Theoretical foundations	Y?	N?
Psychology	Y?	N?
Research	Y?	N?
Have goals	Y?	N?
Follow a method	Y?	N?
External evaluation criteria	Y?	N?
Diagnosis and treatment	Y?	N?
Clients know what they need	Y?	N?
Primacy given to autonomy	Y?	N?
Political, economic, social and technological contexts	N?	Y?

less about acquiring new skills and more about attempting to be clearer about how our clients and we are in our beings?

Turning to examine each of the terms within 'critical existential-analytic psychotherapies', it is evident that there are several influences on the notion of '**critical**' (Loewenthal, 2015a). Psychotherapists could be critical of their theories (and indeed of theory itself). Unfortunately, psychotherapy trainings usually appear to be based on their various gurus, each claiming to have the only truth. It is rare for any of the hundreds of them to encourage being questioned, yet evidence-based research is not necessarily the panacea. It also appears rare for such trainings to have substantial, if sometimes any, critical concerns, for example in terms of the social consequences of psychotherapy; how psychotherapy constructs sexual difference and/or is used to promote class and national interests; the politics of psychotherapeutic truths, and so on (Loewenthal and Campbell, 1998). A further sense of 'critical' comes from the Frankfurt School of critical theory (see Gaitanidis, 2015), which can also be seen more broadly, and sometimes alternatively, in terms of the social, economic and ideological conditions which can cause people's wretchedness. The lack of such explorations is all too common in the various therapeutic trainings which appear not to consider that they have a responsibility to educate trainees in such influences; instead, many can be seen as only considering psychotherapy as assisting in terms of perhaps a liberal type of 'hand up rather than hand out' New Deal that in 1933–39 was Roosevelt's response to what was economically (and could have psychologically been) named the 'Great Depression'.

Regarding '**existential**', aspects such as being in despair or anxious that one is going to die are often taken as existential concerns but surely that shouldn't mean this can only be expressed and explored in what might be seen as at best some nostalgic existential 1950s/60s self-centred modernistic straight-jacket! Thus, as has been argued elsewhere (Loewenthal, 2017), existential psychotherapy and counselling have become stuck and are less likely to have the 'astonishing' and 'changing' (Heaton, 1990) essences of existentialism and are far more likely to be apolitical. Hence the suggestion of the notion of 'post-existentialism' (Loewenthal, 2011), where the implications of thinkers such as Heidegger and Merleau-Ponty might be considered, together with other possibilities including those that argue for the privileging not just of autonomy but being subject-to, for example, ethics, language, writing and an unconscious through, for example, Levinas, Lacan, Derrida and Freud.

Indeed, in referring to Freud, the next term in this Introduction's title is **'analytic'**. This not only refers to existential practices claiming that they are also 'analytic' but to psychoanalysis itself. What is regarded as important here is that existential concerns come first: they are privileged over psychoanalytic ones. There are also such questions as: whose psychoanalysis, to what extent, and how? This is in addition to sometimes difficult questions as to when is psychoanalysis unnecessary and a violence and when are we at best sanitising psychoanalysis because of our own defences as psychotherapists?

The last term in our title is **'psychotherapies'**. Here we are influenced by, for example, Plato's concern that whilst science and technology are important, we have to be continually reminded that therapeia is primarily about the resources of the human soul (Cushman, 2001). Thus, whilst therapy involves a conversation that can't be had elsewhere, it is nevertheless a conversation, and as Gadamer (2013) points out, you can't plan a conversation. Also, the term 'psychotherapies' is deliberately given in the plural as it is acknowledged that there can be many different ways of privileging the implications of the assertions given at the start of this Introduction. Such perspectives have very different assumptions about practice, theory and research. These will now be considered each in turn.

It has been suggested that Freud, Klein, et al (Heaton, 2013; Loewenthal, 2011; Wittgenstein, 1998) tended more towards discovering **practices** from which they subsequently tried to construct theories. Yet most trainings expect their resulting therapists to start from a theoretical place and apply knowledge derived increasingly, and more often exclusively, from empirical research. Thus, such CPD events as working with abandonment may be unhelpful if considered as an application of theory.

Whilst we are interested in **theory**, not least for the possibilities it can open up, it is different if it comes to mind when with the client as an implication but not if we start with it as an application. Merleau-Ponty's (1962) notion of phenomenology being about what emerges in the in-between can be helpful here. Further, if one also accepts that therapeutic knowledge is more about a tacit dimension (Polyani, 1966) which cannot be so much taught and learnt but sometimes might be imparted and acquired, a more sceptical (Heaton, 1993) notion of theory is considered healthier. Nevertheless, theories are very important in being able to open up different possibilities for our practices. For example, if one were to consider the job description of a psychotherapist through what has been attributed to Ricoeur (1965) as the 'hermeneutics of suspicion', this opens up possibilities for the psychotherapist to interpret what could be seen as cover stories that imprison our clients sexually, morally and through capitalism with the help of the likes of Freud, Nietzsche and Marx. To which we might now add therapeutic imprisonment by the state (Loewenthal, Ness and Hardy, 2020).

Overall, hasn't **research** in the psychotherapies moved from any attempt at thoughtful practice to previously being theory driven to currently being based on false notions of evidence-based practice (see for example the introductory debate in Loewenthal and Avdi, 2019)? The above would suggest a different approach to psychotherapy to that currently purported by those that wish to be totally reliant on so-called evidence-based practice. To give an example (which is explored further in several chapters of this book), a more liberally minded evidence-based practitioner might be interested in what is termed 'phenomenological research'; but isn't this a misnomer?

For those who privilege practice, **phenomenology** has provided its own theoretical implications. Leaving aside the question of whose phenomenology, for example, that of Husserl, Heidegger, Merleau-Ponty, Levinas, or Montaigne, in our current more 'evidence-based' era, phenomenology is primarily considered through what it is argued is a misnomer: '**phenomenological research**'. For example, there is the descriptive phenomenological psychological method (Giorgi and Giorgi, 2017), interpretative phenomenological analysis (Smith, Flowers and Larkin, 2009), heuristics (Moustakas, 1990), and so on. Here, various individual accounts are brought together through these different techniques in an attempt to find common phenomena. Yet even if this is possible, can it really help other psychotherapists? Even more importantly, doesn't this psychologising of phenomenology unhelpfully detract from the original notions of phenomenology: surely phenomenology *is* research? (Loewenthal, 2015b). Yet it is currently increasingly unlikely that students of the psychological therapies will consider an aspect of interest being explored/researched in the style of, for example, Kierkegaard, Nietzsche, Montaigne, Heidegger, among others.

Perhaps even more calamitous is the fact that the phenomenological description arising from a single case study, which we might call psychotherapy's traditional approach to research stemming from phusis/physis (it is the natural and what comes out itself), is no longer allowed. This is because trending consumer legislation means that case studies can no longer just be anonymised, but instead the client/patient has to give written consent for the actual article, beyond what is common for ethics approval and for unspecified publication. Hence, the client/patient has to read the to-be-published account of his/her therapist and agree that it has been appropriately anonymised. In actuality, this means that most previously trained psychotherapists are unlikely to consider it ethical or therapeutically helpful for their client/patient. Thus, the life blood of psychotherapy has lost being able to show publicly what has been its own way of doing research. It has been taken away and driven underground. There is an argument that 'effective psychotherapy' should be on the edges of our culture; but we have then to accept our place there and not so much as part of the establishment.

A further related catastrophe is the current fashion in psychotherapeutic research, which has moved away from considering the implications, for example, of what certain existential philosophies might have made of a particular researcher's question. Rather, theory is primarily used to justify concepts (increasingly as technologies) by showing how its application can be empirically evidenced. In fact, it would increasingly appear that the tail is wagging the dog, in that only those theoretical ideas that would appear to be able to be researched, usually more quantitatively than qualitatively, will be considered.

It is argued that in this way, questions of practices, theories and research have been increasingly thrown out of alignment with what might otherwise be taken as the nature of therapeutic knowledge, including its tacit dimensions, despite some attempts elsewhere through scholars such as Lave (1991) and Lave and Wenger (1991) to return to it. What, if anything, can be done? Some possibilities are provided by this book; however, before introducing the chapters, a brief word as to how this particular publication was initiated.

This book came about because of an unprecedented, in the previous 21 years of the *European Journal of Psychotherapy and Counselling*, processing crisis. As a result, I very much brought forward this project which was destined to be a book. Hence, my colleagues and doctoral and masters students, all of whom are involved in our critical existential-analytic psychotherapy training (SAFPAC. co.uk), immediately rallied round and the journal's special issue was published, with the title: *Critical Existential Analytic, Rather Than 'Evidence Based', Psychotherapies: Some Implications for Practices, Theories and Research* (Loewenthal, 2020b). Now this book has finally appeared, developed from this special issue. My thanks also to our three published respondents and especially the *EJPC* editorial team: Dr Evrinomy Avdi, Dr Anastasios Gaitanidis, Dr Jay Watts and Prof David Winter and to our departing Assistant Editor, Laura Scott-Rosales; their assistance with this special issue went far beyond their usual 'beyond the call of duty'! Further thanks for their invaluable assistance with this special issue to: Dr Gauri Beecroft, Dr Christian Buckland, Dr Linda Finlay, Dr Sacha Lawrence, Dr Seth Osborne and Sally Parsloe.

I will now turn to introduce the chapters:

Chapter 1 is by Onel Brooks, entitled *Looking like a foreigner: Foreignness, conformity and compliance in psychoanalysis*. As one reviewer commented, 'this is a stimulating paper, I found it of particular interest that it appeared to challenge the notion of psychoanalysis as a science, therefore the analyst having superiority over the analysand and others... The personal examples of foreignness were illuminating, especially in the light of one being a client example and one being from the author's, personal, lived experience'.

Chapter 2 is *Language as Gesture in Merleau-Ponty: Some implications for method in therapeutic practice and research* by Julia Cayne. As another reviewer commented, 'a very interesting and well thought through piece... I really enjoyed your interpretations of in-between Lacan and Merleau-Ponty... [and] the parallels between Merleau-Ponty's and Winnicott's notions of the "spontaneous gesture"'.

In Chapter 3, *The private life of meaning – some implications for psychotherapy and psychotherapeutic research*, Tony McSherry (as lead author), Del Loewenthal and Julia Cayne explore questions arising from a study concerning how mental health nurses are therapeutic. As a reviewer commented, 'I found it extremely interesting and refreshing to read about the authors' reflections... and this relates to phenomenology and truthfulness. I specifically enjoyed the authors' openness and the exploration surrounding dispelling one's own assumptions and beliefs in order to reduce the possibilities of closing something important down and for people to sit with the uncomfortable feelings attached to not knowing'.

Regarding Chapter 4 by Elizabeth Nicholl (as lead author), Del Loewenthal and James Davies, *Finding my voice: Telling stories with heuristic self-search inquiry*, a reviewer commented: 'it is well written... a particular strength of the paper is in its innovative methodology, as well as the fact that it provides an engaging and experience-near account of the first author's transformative and later painful experience of disclosing her diagnosis in therapy during her psychotherapy training'.

Chapter 5, '*When working in a youth service, how do therapists experience humour with their clients?*' by Patricia Talens has been described as 'well written and fascinating'. The reviewer further commented that 'this article begins with a thoughtful story in literature regarding therapeutic practice and follows... [with an] exploration of how the author conducted their research and ends with an honest critique'.

Chapter 6, our final chapter before introducing the published respondents, is *What gets in the way of working with clients who have been sexually abused? Heuristic inquiry* by Iana Trichkova (as lead author), Del Loewenthal, Betty

Bertrand and Catherine Altson. This chapter is further described by a reviewer as one that 'presents a study using heuristic inquiry which was stimulated by the primary researcher's experiences of working with clients who have been sexually abused'. In fact, our first published respondent described it as '… stop[ping] me in my tracks. Not only because of the shocking, disturbing and painful content directly evoking a range of feelings within me. Not only because of the crystal-clear clarity, competence and attention to detail with which the article is written. It is also a great example of the effectiveness of heuristic inquiry when it is done properly'.

That first respondent is Manu Bazzano, who might be seen as coming from a more existential perspective. In Chapter 7, *Maculate conceptions*, Manu considers the series of papers that both provide a refreshing ambivalence at the heart of psychoanalysis and are effective in opening explorations to post-qualitative investigations.

Our second respondent is Laura Chernaik, who might be seen as coming from a more psychoanalytic perspective. In Chapter 8, entitled *The pictures you paint in the stories you tell, a response*, Laura is interested in 'intention' and argues for approaching critique heterotopically, with an emphasis on other worlds and the relation of these to subjectivity and the unconscious.

Our third and final published response is from Steen Halling, who might be seen as coming from a more phenomenological perspective. Chapter 9 is entitled *Reflections on the tensions between openness and method in experientially oriented research and psychotherapy*. In this chapter, Steen addresses issues around the challenges of using phenomenological methods and studying phenomena systematically whilst retaining an attitude of humility.

Chapter 10, *On the very idea of post-existentialism*, by Del Loewenthal is the final chapter. Here, I attempt to say more about post-existentialism, my forerunner to the term critical existential-analytic. My aims are as follows: firstly, to consider the implications for therapeutic practice of the writings of such existentialists as Kierkegaard and Heidegger – without being caught up in what had seemed to become existentialism's inferred narcissism. Secondly, to reopen question of politics and ideology in our practices. Thirdly, to re-privilege Merleau-Ponty's phenomenology in attempting to always start with what emerges between client and practitioner, rather than to start with specific theories. Finally, to provide a space in which structural linguistics and various post-modern writers can be considered as having possible implications for our practices.

Overall, I am attempting, with particular reference to existentialism and psychoanalysis, to outline through this book some ways in which psychotherapies might be able to move away from the crisis mainly caused by what is currently wrongly being taken as the nature of psychotherapeutic knowledge, as exemplified by the 'evidence-based practice' movement. In summary, I have suggested instead: a primacy being given to practice, considering theories as having implications rather than applications, and privileging thoughtfulness with notions of research being seen more as cultural practices.

Of course, there are very likely to be those who would insist that the approaches influenced by the assumptions given in this Introduction should first be researched as to whether they are indeed proper evidence-based practices; but, that depends on what one takes to be the nature of psychotherapeutic knowledge!

References

Cushman, R. (2001). *Therapeia: Plato's Conception of Philosophy* (new ed.). Piscataway, NJ: Transaction.

Gadamer, H-G. (2013). *Truth and Method*. London: Bloomsbury Academic.

Gaitanidis, A. (2015). Critical Theory and Psychotherapy. In D. Loewenthal (Ed.), *Critical Psychotherapy, Psychoanalysis and Counselling: Implications for Practice*. London: Routledge. pp. 95–107.

Giorgi, M. and Giorgi, B. (2017). Phenomenological Psychology. In C. Willig and W. Rogers (Eds.), *The Sage Handbook of Qualitative Research in Psychology*. Thousand Oaks, CA: Sage. pp. 165–178.

Heaton, J. (1990). 'What is Existential Analysis?' *Journal of the Society for Existential Analysis*, 1(1): 2–6.

Heaton, J. M. (1993). The Sceptical Tradition in Psychotherapy. In L. Spurling (Ed.), *From the Words of My Mouth: Tradition in Psychotherapy*. London: Routledge. pp. 106–131.

Heaton, J. (2013). *The Talking Cure: Wittgenstein on Language as Bewitchment and Clarity*. Basingstoke: Palgrave Macmillan.

Lave, J. (1991). Situated Learning in Communities of Practice. In L. B. Resnick, J. M. Levine and S. D. Teasley (Eds.), *Perspectives on Socially Shared Cognition*. Washington, D.C.: American Psychological Association. pp. 63–82.

Lave, J. and Wenger, E. (1991). *Situated Learning: Legitimate Peripheral Participation*. Cambridge: Cambridge University Press.

Loewenthal, D. and Campbell, R. (1998). The Contest of European Meaning. *European Journal of Psychotherapy, Counselling and Health*, 1(2): 177–181.

Loewenthal, D. (2011). *Post-Existentialism and the Psychological Therapies: Towards a Therapy without Foundations*. London: Karnac.

Loewenthal, D. (2015a). *Critical Psychotherapy, Psychoanalysis and Counselling: Implications for Practice*. London: Routledge.

Loewenthal, D. (2015b). What Have Current Notions of Psychotherapeutic Research to do with Truth, Justice and Thoughtful Practice? *European Journal of Psychotherapy & Counselling*, 17(1): 1–4.

Loewenthal, D. (2017). *Existential Psychotherapy and Counselling after Postmodernism: The Selected Works of Del Loewenthal*. Hove: Routledge World Library of Mental Health.

Loewenthal, D. and Avdi, E. (2019). Introduction. In D. Loewenthal and E. Avdi (Eds.), *Developments in Psychotherapeutic Qualitative Research*. London: Routledge. pp. 1–11.

Loewenthal, D. (2020a). Existential Therapeutic Practice After Post-Modernism. In M. Bazzano (Ed.), *Re-visioning Existential Therapy: Counter-Traditional Perspectives*. London: Routledge. pp. 248–260.

Loewenthal, D. (2020b). Critical Existential-Analytic, Rather Than 'Evidence Based', Psychotherapies: Some Implications for Practices, Theories and Research. *Special Issue, European Journal of Psychotherapy and Counselling*, 22: 1–2.

Loewenthal, D., Ness, O. and Hardy, B. (2020). *Beyond the Therapeutic State*. London: Routledge.
Merleau-Ponty, M. (1962). *The Phenomenology of Perception*. London: Routledge.
Moustakas, C. E. (1990). *Heuristic Research: Design, Methodology, and Applications*. Newbury Park, California: Sage Publications, Inc.
Polyani, M. (1966). *The Tacit Dimension*. New York: Doubleday.
Ricoeur, P. (1965). *History and Truth*. Evanston, IL: Northwestern University Press.
Smith, J., Flowers, P. and Larkin, M. (2009). *Interpretative Phenomenological Analysis*. London: Sage.
Wittgenstein, L. (1998). *Culture and Value* (2nd ed.) (P. Winch, Trans.; G.H. von Right, in collaboration with Heikki Nyman, revised by Alios Pichler, Eds.) Oxford: Blackwell.

Looking like a foreigner: Foreignness, conformity and compliance in psychoanalysis

Onel Brooks

ABSTRACT
This paper suggests that to approach another person confident that we are in possession of 'universally applicable' concepts and ideas is to begin in the wrong place both with that person and our ideas. It is to begin as someone who is well armed, well trained and perhaps too focused on succeeding by finding what she is looking for. Looking carefully at the particular, looking like a foreigner who has never seen what is before her is contrasted with looking like someone who is concerned with conquest and domination. In particular, this paper takes a sceptical view of the claim or assumption that psychoanalysis is 'universally applicable' and that a training in psychoanalysis prepares a practitioner to engage thoughtfully and honestly with race and culture. It argues that although psychoanalysis tends to treat race and culture as if they are marginal and optional, in its theorising, its practice and history psychoanalysis betrays the fact that race, culture and the treatment of what is regarded as foreign are central and fundamental to it.

Introduction

Thirty years ago it was common practice to run psychoanalytic trainings, giving very little consideration to race, culture, class, history and the socio-political context in which we work. Has this changed? Now, after four or five years on a more orthodox psychoanalytic training, some of the trainees and those charged with teaching them may, yielding to a lurking disquiet, seek to appease a sense of something being amiss by tacking on a few seminars about race, and or tellingly 'difference' (tellingly because this seems to imply that the training is about sameness) and features of the socio-political context on to the end of what it presents as the really important matter, the transmission of a body of knowledge or thinking called psychoanalysis.

Assumptions and convictions about the universal applicability of psychoanalytic concepts, help to keep this practice plausible and in place. For even if psychoanalysis is not conceived and spoken about as the science of the mind, more orthodox versions of psychoanalysis tend to treat it as a neutral perspective, uncontaminated by race, culture and politics, and these latter matters as peripheral and optional to it. Psychoanalysis, on such an account, finally shows us how all human minds work, and as such is able to tell us all about race and racism too. This seems to privilege psychoanalysis, assuming that it is born standing up and standing back somewhere neutral and clear-sighted, and as such is uncontaminated by issues such as race, culture, history and the socio-political context. This uncontaminated immaculate conception version of what psychoanalysis is, is intimately related to the claim, assumption or conviction that in transmitting and practising psychoanalysis, we can create and inhabit spaces where such considerations are not really so important, because we are concerned with what is 'deeper' than socio-political and historical matters, and because psychoanalysis is 'deeper', those trained in it, being experts on the psyche or 'internal world', are automatically well placed to understand and deal sensitively with most issues, including those that are to do with race, culture and difference generally.

A few comments about what this paper is not may help to clarify what it sets out to be. It may be argued that it is surely a mistake to present contemporary courses in psychoanalysis and contemporary practitioners as having much to do with notions of being in possession of 'the science of the mind'. Fifty or even thirty years ago, yes, but now? And, the argument against this paper might continue, psychoanalysis is not one but many: some schools definitely do not think of themselves in this way. Furthermore, we might know individual psychoanalytic practitioners who do not have this attitude to what they are doing. The claim that this current paper is making is not that this self-conception is often or ever articulated, but that in so far as psychoanalysis and any form of psychotherapy is thought of as the application of a body of knowledge to all people at all times in all places, and without careful attention to time, place and the particularities of the people involved, including class, race, culture, gender, it is trading on, exploiting, making thoughtful or thoughtless use of the cultural trope of the scientist or the expert (who is closely related to the scientist). Psychoanalysis, other forms of psychotherapy, literature, film, and life in general might teach us that what people say is one thing, but it is wise to also pay attention to what they do. It is important to keep it in mind that the acrimonious 'controversial discussions', touched on below, which took place in the 1940 were conducted in 'scientific meetings' and that from London to New York to San Francisco, New England and Toronto, psychoanalytic organisations still refer to their meetings as 'scientific meetings'.

There is a vast literature of thoughtful engagement with psychoanalysis, drawing on philosophy, commenting on the schisms and power plays in psychoanalysis, and on its failures when it comes to gender, race, class. This paper would be impossibly longer if it tried to say something about thoughtful and political engagement with psychoanalysis both in Britain and the United States, including 'the interpersonalists', 'the relational school' and 'turn', R D Laing, the Philadelphia Association, anti-psychiatry and critical psychiatry, Jaffa Kareem, Roland Littlewood and the work of the Women's Therapy Centre in London (See Cushman, 2015; Lowe, 2013; Orbach, 2007; Stern & Hirsch, 2017) These individuals and organisations have had a profound influence on the author of this paper. However, the argument being made here is that after all this, this practicing, writing and speaking, it is still the case that there are courses in psychoanalysis which tack on a seminar or two about 'race' or 'difference' onto itself, as if what is essential to psychoanalysis has little or nothing to do with race, difference, and the political context in which we live and practice.

This paper, then, is more lament than a review of the literature. For, in spite of this body of literature, there is still an inveterate belief in psychoanalysis as something universal, like a science, something that in some ways floats freely from culture.

Inspiration or echoes for this paper might be found in Derrida and Duformentalle (2000), Kristeva (1991), Levinas (1969), and Levinas & Kearney (1984), as well as in the work of Adam Phillips, and Bracken and Thomas (2005). This paper agrees with Adam Phillips comment that we might be disinclined 'to believe that because a person has done a recognized or legitimated official training they are then qualified to claim something more than that they have done the training (doing something properly is a way of not doing it differently)' (Phillips, 1997, p. xiv). Courses are good at getting people to speak or even believe in a particular language game, in seeing things in the ways that the celebrated others see things, in keeping people seeing in the same way. On the other hand, psychoanalysis, when it is not a matter of political positioning -presenting itself as closer to medicine or 'science'- when it is not insisting on its superiority to other ways of thinking, when it is not a champion of conformity, an implicit or explicit system for distinguishing between 'normal' and 'deviant', it might be a way of reminding us that in spite of our desire to present ourselves as consistent with ourselves, as consistent with the culturally dominant conception of what it is to be a good person, to cast ourselves as commensurate with the other people around us (or maybe only the important ones), psychoanalysis might be part of a reminder that and of how we are at odds with ourselves, with the people around us, an invitation to our foreignness (Phillips 1997: xv). The contrast here is between seeing psychoanalysis as doing and seeing in the same authorised way, in order to conform, pass the training, be recognised as belonging, as a bona fide citizen of the state referred to as 'psychoanalysis', and on the other hand, the claim that what is of most value in psychoanalysis is a welcome to, a celebration of foreigners, and encouraging us to look like foreigners.

What follows is an attempt to provoke us to think more about the practice of tacking on a seminar or two about race and culture or 'difference' onto the supposedly foundational and universally valid body of knowledge called 'psychoanalysis'. The paper argues that notions of race and culture are often present but evaded, neglected and obscured in psychoanalysis, and that this sort of neglect, evasion and not seeing is tied up with notions about who and what belongs where, who is in charge of psychoanalysis and, therefore, the right way to think. Looking like a foreigner, then, is related to the ability to look at psychoanalysis like a foreigner, which is the very thing that success on most trainings must threaten, as trainings offers us a way of looking like one of us, an insider, as opposed to one of them, an outsider. According to this line of thinking, then, training in psychoanalysis, especially versions which tempt us to universalise and think of ourselves as 'applying' psychoanalysis, is excellent for helping to destroy our capacity to do what may be of most value in psychoanalysis: our ability to provide welcome to what is strange, foreign and potentially unsettling in ourselves and others, what we have never heard or thought of.

Conquests and compromises

'I am not at all a man of science, not an observer, not an experimenter, not a thinker. I am by temperament nothing but a conquistador' (Szasz, 2006, p. 33). This is what Freud, a man who had to flee from the Nazis, told his friend Wilhelm Fliess. It is possible perhaps to dismiss this, but Freud himself is one of our teachers when it comes to helping us to pay attention and think about what is in front of us, to be less dismissive. If Freud likens himself to the Spanish and Portuguese explorer-soldiers, professional warriors who conquered much of the world for Spain and Portugal during the sixteenth, seventeenth and eighteenth centuries, might we not wonder whether psychoanalysis might be regarded as a form of conquest, domination? We do not have to say that this is what psychoanalysis always is. This would be a generalisation rather than the acknowledgement of a possibility, tendency or temptation. Why would we want to generalise from one of Freud's comments and pronounce something about all psychoanalysis at all times in all situations? As well as the notion of conquest, dominating and overpowering, this remark of Freud's might remind us of race and culture, of how Europe has plundered, massacred, enslaved and dominated the foreign others it has encountered. This might lead us to wonder whether the way we treat the foreign others is related to how we treat the foreigners that we might glimpse or meet in ourselves.

Writing to Edward Glover in 1940 about the fierce ideological battle between Mrs Klein and Miss Freud, which later became 'the controversial discussions' James Strachey states that 'if it comes to a showdown – I'm very strongly in favour of compromise at all cost' (Rayner, 1994, p. 18). By 1940 it was known that the Nazi regime was murdering people it considered to be subhuman, due to ethnicity, race, sexuality, as well as other undesirable outsiders, such as its political opponents and those regarded as 'mentally ill'. This paper is concerned with foreignness, with seeing someone or something as foreign, and with looking like a foreigner. It is difficult not to think about 'compromise at all cost' in this context. How can Strachey be so uncompromising about compromising? Is it an extreme position to be uncompromisingly compromising? Is compromising always a good thing, and do we not have to consider what compromising might cost us, or what we compromise by being so willing to compromise? I fear that in the face of the two extremes represented in his letter by Mrs Klein and Miss Freud, Strachey's 'compromise at all cost' might be regarded as another extreme position: that in the face of dogma, he has taken a dogmatic position about compromising.

Strachey continues

> These attitudes on both sides are of course purely religious and the very antithesis of science. They are also (on both sides) infused by, I believe, a desire to dominate the situation and in particular the future – which is why both sides lay so much stress on the training of candidates. Actually, of course, it's megalomanic mirage to suppose that you can control the opinion of the people you analyse beyond a certain limited point. But in any case it ought naturally to be the aim of a training analysis to put the trainee into a position to arrive at his own decisions upon moot points – not to stuff him with your own private dogma. (Rayner, 1994, p. 18)

These comments and observations may lead us to other comments and observations, beginning with the remark that both religion and science might be said to be fond of claiming 'universal application' or applicability, and that this has been, at times at least, a first step in demanding that others comply, do as we do, believe as we believe. To say something like this is not to go along with Strachey's attempt to contrast religion and science in this way: it is to say that religion and science are in some ways not so foreign to each other. Second, psychoanalysis is presented here as at least sometimes yielding to temptations to dominate and control the views of others, passing on shared and private dogma whilst claiming to be engaged in something 'scientific'. Such comments and observations may lead us to wonder how we might approach psychoanalysis so that it is not a matter of passing on shared or private dogma, constructing and bequeathing a set of truths about all human beings in all times and all places, discrediting and excommunicating those who do not comply with our version of what psychoanalysis is.

To continue with Strachey's letter, he writes, 'Why should these wretched fascists and (bloody foreigners) communists invade our peaceful compromising land?' (Rayner, 1994, p. 18). My worry is that the image of the 'wretched fascists and (bloody foreigners) communists invading our peaceful', idyllic, democratic and 'compromising land' is part of the problem. It is as if Britain did not have an empire, as if peaceful, idyllic, democratic, compromising and rather charming is not only one side of the story.

It is not just that at the time of Strachey's writing these words there is a war on and the people he refers to have fled from fascists threats to their lives for being 'bloody foreigners' no matter how long they have lived in Germany. It is not just that this idyllic picture of our democratic compromising land does seem to be a little idealised, and what you see if you do not look like a foreigner. For instance, Rayner tells us that 'Glover, one of the main protagonists in the quarrel' -hardly a refugee from Nazi Germany- 'was disliked for his high-handed and anti-democratic running of the Society'. Ernest Jones had created the Society in 1920 and then ran it 'autocratically' for twenty-seven years. This seems to be part of the 'peaceful compromising land' the 'bloody foreigners' threaten by their presence. 'Compromise at any cost' seems to have much to do with keeping things the way we are used to them, keeping them familiar. Rayner writes, 'Why this was tolerated by the membership for so long is an interesting question' (Rayner, 1994, p. 19). Indeed! Practitioners and trainees familiar with psychoanalysis easily ask themselves about compliance and conformity when it comes to institutions, organisations and families. We should not stop short of asking a similar question about psychoanalysis. Is there something about psychoanalytic trainings, authority and orthodoxy that inclines those who have undergone such trainings to fear rocking the boat and being seen as foreigners when it comes to psychoanalysis? Does this help us to understand why for twenty-seven years psychoanalysts put up with, went along with autocratic rule? There are often anxieties that change, doing things differently, including those who are usually excluded, will lead to chaos, anarchy, panic. Often it is easy to increase our anxieties about such matters and manipulate us. It is not clear that being trained in psychoanalysis significantly addresses such anxieties, provokes thoughtfulness, or makes us less vulnerable to manipulation and mystification about such matters.

And we need to state the obvious sometimes: there could be no psychoanalytic society without the people referred to in this letter as 'wretched fascists and (bloody foreigners)'.

Modernism and universal application

To insist on seeing psychoanalysis as having 'universal application', as the science of the mind, may be seen as part of and thus a way of continuing the modernist project: the attitude and conviction that the West is naturally superior because it has made use of reason to sweep away superstition, custom and empty stupidity that many cultures and peoples are still caught up in (West, 1996, pp. 7-16). But can modernism be considered as neutral about race and culture? Clearly it knows too much about who is superior to whom and, therefore should control and dominate. Writing about modernism, Bracken and Thomas state, 'Proponents of this idea maintained that all the problems of our lives on this planet would ultimately yield to scientific investigation and to the application of one sort of technology or another' (Bracken & Thomas, 2005, p. 6). Modernism then looks to science and technology as the way to salvation for all our human ills. A modernist way of thinking about psychoanalysis is to see it as a technology that may save us. Those who are critical of modernist ways of approaching psychoanalysis are suspected of being willfully ignorant, stupid or perverse. That is, they are outside of and foreign to the place we occupy: we who are reasonable.

However, it is also possible to take another view of what psychoanalysis is and might be able to help us with, a view that is more questioning and takes less for granted, that is more curious and attentive to our hopes and aspirations for psychoanalysis. It might help us to ask about our attitudes and convictions when it comes to psychoanalysis, what our insisting might be about, what this fixation on science and technology might be doing to us, as well as preventing us from doing. Such a view of psychoanalysis may be part of being preoccupied with our 'limits and limitations' -rather than the rational ego's conquest of the irrational and unconscious- and may be seen as continuous with such preoccupations from Sophocles through to Kierkegaard, Nietzsche and Wittgenstein. Postmodernism, then, might be regarded as an attempt to come to terms with the 'limits and limitations' of modernism, a way of raising and living with the 'doubts, uncertainties and anxieties' which are the cost associated with modernity. It does not have to be a rejection of the Enlightenment or its children -psychoanalysis, Marxism and liberalism, 'It simply rejects their claim to be foundational and universally valid' (Bracken & Thomas, 2005, p. 7). 'Postmodernism' might be used as a term for arguing and indicating that our thoughts, actions, practices, needs and desires are interrelated, so no part of how we live can be isolated and held up as foundational and universally valid. Claims and convictions about the universal application of psychoanalysis easily come from inside modernism, a term for the attitudes, assumptions and convictions the West has had since the sixteenth century about what the West is and how it is superior to other peoples and cultures: 'postmodernism' can be a name for an attempt to escape from and think about such assumptions and convictions. Many philosophers and psychotherapists have made use of postmodernism to help us think about psychotherapy including psychoanalysis (Loewenthal, 2011; Loewenthal and Snell, 2003; Parker, 1999), but rather than explore the literature, I turn to my own experiences.

Some illustrations

So far, this paper has had something to say about the history of psychoanalysis and of Europe, and taking a superior attitude to those outsiders identified as foreigners. Here are some examples that are more personal and contemporary, which are perhaps more revealing against the historical background referred to above. My first illustration is of a discussion with a psychoanalytic colleague in which I claim that there is a difference between the term and concept, on the one hand, and on the other, what the term or concept refers to. I say that the 'inner world', for example, is a concept. He stops me to say, 'Everyone has an internal world, One!'. I was making a point about systems of beliefs, how questions and comments can come from within or from outside such systems, and saying that it is possible to take a look at psychoanalytic concepts as part of a system of ideas that arose in and therefore is a part of western European culture. The issue is not whether people have, feelings, desires, thoughts, inclinations, fantasies, and so on, that they may or may not express. (I certainly do not want to argue against this.) We might say from within psychoanalysis that 'of course everyone has an internal world, or an unconscious or an Oedipus complex', but this is to speak from inside and perhaps affirm a right to apply psychoanalysis. We might notice that this is not dissimilar to insisting from inside another system of belief that we all have an 'immortal souls' and need to be 'saved'. Psychoanalysis as insisting on asserting psychoanalytic concepts is perhaps not as interesting or important as psychoanalysis as a way of helping us to become interested in the need to insist and affirm, and in what might happen or become open to us, if we insisted less and knew less.

My second illustration brings together two sorts of experiences. The first sort of experience is that I have been stopped as I am walking through a train by someone who wants to tell me that the air conditioning is not working or that the toilet is broken. The embarrassed person then tells me that it is because I am wearing a white shirt or because I am in a jacket that they made the mistake of thinking I must be the train guard. I tend to be unconvinced by this. Perhaps this is because I am someone who is often regarded as 'foreign', 'different' and 'other' in the country where I have lived most of my life. Something similar and different has happened to me in groups of psychoanalysts who have had an orthodox training. Something is said about where I trained and I am asked 'But are you psychoanalytic?' As I attempt to formulate something about how there might be different ways of understanding what 'being psychoanalytic' means, the questioner specifies what she means. 'Do you work with the negative transference?' Again my mouth opens but she has no interest in what might come out of it, because she knows what psychoanalysis is. It is as she and the people who think like her say it is. A particular view of psychoanalysis is presented as if it must be the view of what psychoanalysis is; those with other views are 'other'.

I am not suggesting that my racial and cultural differences were dealt with by being displaced onto issues to do with who really belongs in psychoanalysis. I am taking my colleague at or close to her word. For it is possible and all too often evident that someone who refers to herself as psychoanalytic can disparage others who live and work with psychoanalysis. The one who disparages seems to know that the other person cannot be psychoanalytic because they clearly do not belong in the right subgroup or tribe. And yet this practitioner does not see how this is similar to situations where race and class prejudices are evident.

One of the things that interest me is our tendency to perceive, designate and create 'foreignness', so the foreign other, desire or self can be excluded and regarding as wrong, dangerous or at least a little ridiculous. That and how we do this to other people, to our thoughts, desires and acts, to ourselves, is, I am arguing, fundamental to what happens in many consulting rooms. Once we have the orthodox or approved or authoritative form of anything, we have those who do not conform, the deviants, those who must be kept out. Once I have an orthodox and approved view of who or what I am, there will be aspect of me that do not fit this picture, so will need to be treated as foreign and kept out. This is to create an inside, a border and border controls; it is to create 'foreigners'. Our dreams, fantasies and fleeting thoughts indicate the extent to which we also belong to another world or other persons live within us. We might say that psychoanalysis teaches us that foreign lands and peoples are never far away, and we may locate our fear of foreignness in some foreigners somewhere, as we look away from how we are strangers and foreigners to ourselves. Is it ironic to say that someone might be caught up in keeping what is foreign out in their professional political life, yet in their work with clients, they are concerned with welcoming and exploring what is foreign?

My third illustration is a comment made to me by a client. She tells me that since she has been in therapy with me she has not been happier. She does however feel that her life is better. She is more thoughtful, more aware of what she is feeling, more able to see the dances that she gets into with people and with herself. She grins and claims that she knows that it is ridiculous and part of the culture that everything needs to be efficient and clear, but she still wants me to make a diagnosis, set out clearly what is wrong with her, and give her some bullet points about what she needs to do. For her, sometimes at least, 'a better life' may not be as appealing as 'happiness' and something that she can apply, something that by-passes the trance like, seance like, charged but uncertain intimacies of our sessions. She would sometimes rather that psychoanalysis was more about the application of a technology than about intimacy and ethics. For her therapist though, intimacy and ethics must come before technology.

Here is a more substantial illustration of some of the issues I am trying to raise and explore rather than solve.

Client example

I go to collect my client from the waiting room for his first session. There is only one person in the waiting room. I say my name and ask if he has come to see me. He looks rather unsure and a little worried, but he gets up and comes into the consulting room with me. He is white, athletic, casually dressed and not very talkative. I try to give him ways of beginning to speak to me – saying how long the session is, encouraging him to begin wherever he want to. However, he wants to know what I know about him. I have long forgotten the referral form I read about two weeks ago, and say that I would rather hear directly from him. He is quiet. He then asks me about football. I talk to him about football. He soon notices that my knowledge of football is limited. He is amused by this. Then he lapses into silence for a while. I do not yet have any idea what I may need to do in this session. I sit with him in silence. I cannot say whether this helps or frustrates, but he begins to tell me about himself.

He is a working class lad from a poor family who did very well academically, winning a scholarship to a prestigious school where most of the pupils are very rich and tend to flaunt their wealth, social position, and their sense of being destined to rule. They spoke incessantly about their houses – usually they had several- cars – usually they had several – yachts – usually they had several, and their lavish holidays abroad – usually they had several a year. Because they ridiculed 'poor people', the 'working classes' and 'foreigners', and often arranged to go to each others' houses in the breaks, Adam found himself trying to keep to himself, for fear of being humiliated. Surely humiliation would follow from any of them visiting the ramshackle little house he lived in with his mother. His fear of this kind of exposure and ridicule fed his tendency to say little to 'them'. He made friends with a few of the rebellious and delinquent boys who were lucky or unlucky enough to find themselves in a school where they felt that they did not fit in. He developed a reputation of being a demon on the sports pitch, as well as the sort of boy who does not hesitate to take on a group of boys in a fist fight, inflicting more damage on the group than they collectively are able to inflict on him. This was a clear message to 'them', the majority of rich arrogant and condescending boys that they messed with him at their peril.

I said little, but I acknowledged that what he told me sounded hard to bear, and remarked that I was not surprised that he might have been angry and rebellious at that school. I also commented on his hesitation when I introduced myself. He said that he had expected to see a woman. He thought all or nearly all counsellors and therapists were women.

He came for all of his sessions. It seemed important for him to talk and for me to allow him to do so. He had not really told anyone the whole story before; he tended to present himself as the sort of boy who talks a little about football but does not say much. When he found himself telling me something that had the power to expose him as upset and capable of crying, he became fierce and more Anglo Saxon expressions were pushed out of his mouth. It seemed to be important for me to acknowledge how upsetting and angry making these things were, and not to give him the impression that unless his distress and anger manifested themselves as full blown crying, I could not see them in him.

He told me that an African boy won a scholarship to the school and 'they' gave him hell. Adam befriended the boy. 'He was alright! We got on'. Adam told me that one day he came upon a situation where the African boy was being talked at condescendingly by a small group of boys jeering and laughing at him – a group of 'them'. He heard them say something like, 'So what's the matter with you people? Don't you have food in your country? How comes we are always having to feed you?' Adam waded in and confronted the group of boys who quickly stopped laughing. The boy who seemed to have been the most vocal to the African boy wanted to stand his ground, but his friends wisely pulled him away. Adam said that he was utterly furious with this group of boys and the school where this sort of thing can happen and nobody cares. He was clearly furious and upset when he was telling me.

A boy like Adam tends to polarise opinions and positions. Some of the teachers thought that he was a bad influence on the other boys, too rough and aggressive. They were apparently oblivious to the roughness and aggression of many of the boys there, and to these qualities in the school. Apparently there was little thought that the school could change. In contrast to the group of teachers who could only see his aggression and roughness, there was a group of teachers who liked and got on with Adam. Perhaps they had some sense of why a school like this might be difficult for him. He and his friend, another white lad who felt that he did not fit in, were involved in some football related prank. Something rebellious that did not hurt anyone and was easily put right. He explained to me that although similar pranks usually meant that the boys were called to the Head's office and given a talking to, he and the other boy were expelled, much to the surprise of some of the teachers and the boys' parents. Adam claimed that the Head saw an opportunity to get rid of him and his friend, and grabbed it. His friend and the mothers wept openly when the expulsion was clear and final: Adam was absolutely defiant and unrepentant in front of 'them' and still furious when telling this to me.

At the end of his sessions with me, Adam was in one of the local colleges, getting on with his studies, making friends and relieved that he was not in a school for rich arrogant and cruel boys, and that he no longer stood out so much, and was no longer a target for this subtle and not so subtle aggression. He had in this new environment softened quite a bit.

There are clearly issues to do with race in what is above. The treatment of the African boy does explicitly foreground race and culture. Perhaps Adam being expelled from a very expensive elite school and finding his way into a local college might prompt thoughts about the black boys, as well as the working class white boys who are expelled from school but do not find their way back into the education system. It is possible, though, to say that this account is badly chosen for this occasion as it is about class rather than race, but not to wonder about the possible connections between class and, on the other hand, race and culture.

The reader would be mistaken in thinking that my not giving an account of masculinity, Adam's relationship with his father and his mother means that these matters were not addressed at all. From how he was with me and what he had to say about 'that school', we got onto his difficulties with his father and his thoughts that his being at that school was related to his father's wishes and aspirations. My work with Adam was not an attempt to apply universal applicable concepts and connections: it was more a matter of trying to follow his lead and finding sometimes that some familiar themes emerged. This young man presented himself to the world as strong, athletic, not afraid of violence and not really bothered about anything. He expected all therapists to be women and seemed to struggle with the fact that his experiences at that school had left him with feelings and responses he had worked hard to regard as foreign to him, but native to women. As he had left that environment, he no longer needed to work so hard to make it seem as if such feelings and responses do not belong in him. It is, I argue, no coincidence that 'the working classes' and the 'foreigners' might be lumped together in the way these schoolboys speak. 'Looking like a foreigner', as someone who does not belong or have a right to be there, someone who is vulnerable to many forms of aggression, is what Adam feared. He did not look like a foreigner by having identifiably 'foreign' physical features, such as skin colour, but he feared that something could happen that made him look more like a foreigner than he did already by being working class.

Clearly Adam's history and character were a part of our conversation, and so was his experience of his school that trained conquistadors, the inequalities and injustices that the school seemed to highlight, as well as his indignant refusal to allow the school to violate him further or to be contrite. Far from compromise at any cost, he told me about his constant desperate struggle against a culture or way of being which seemed to rest on the creation, identification and violation of foreigners and foreignness. Such an environment helped to create a rigid version of 'us' 'the normal ones' who are white, male, privileged and destined to rule. Those who are not like us -women, the working class, people without money, black people- will be identified and treated as if they are the ones who have the 'soppy' unacceptable tearful feelings, the ones who are ridiculous and deserve ridicule, the ones who are resourceless and helpless, whilst we have means and are generous. This client example and this paper is not concerned with something called 'intersectionality', with how the overlap of social identities multiplies oppression and creates unique forms of discrimination. This illustration and this paper is about the creation and the maintenance of 'foreignness'. It is not about presenting these schoolboys as reprehensible for being privileged white males who are destined to rule. It touches on the wealthy poverty of the life they find themselves in, the constant effort needed to keep the lines drawn between us and what is foreign, the perpetual parading of privilege that may prevent senses of privation.

Universal application

The example of client work above might prompt us to reflect on how the notion of 'Reason' is tied up with assumptions and views about gender, race and culture. It does not seem to be the case that such assumptions and convictions are long outdated and can be confined to accounts of our past rather than our present. The example above also indicate that privilege, inequalities and a sense of entitlement and being in charge are still with us. We might also reflect on the fact that what came to be said about the rational ego in contrast to the primitive id had and has its sense and power against this motif of the West's self-image. European men (especially the more educated ones, rather than men from the lower classes) rather than women, clearly possessed 'Reason'. There were 'primitive people' and 'civilised people' before psychoanalysis drew up its version of the primitive and the civilised parts of the mind.

Freud writes, 'civilization behaves towards sexuality as a people or a stratum of its population does which has subjected another to its exploitation' (Freud, 1930, p. 746). The West's subjugation and exploitation of others, viewed as too sexual is historically prior to Freud's argument that this is what 'civilised society' does to sexuality. This may be viewed as an account of how civilisation is a matter of trying to make sexuality foreign, and how sexuality, what is forbidden and foreignness may be related.

Ian Parker writes,

It is not merely a historical curiosity that one of Freud's favourite jokes for more than thirty years after first airing, usually prompted when a patient did not appear at the appointed hour, was to say 'twelve o'clock and no negro'. The saying was derived from the caption for a cartoon in a newspaper in 1886 that showed a yawing lion waiting for lunch. This joke, when read alongside Freud' more well-known comment that women's sexuality was a 'dark continent', draws attention to the intertwinement of sex and race in psychoanalysis (Parker, 2012: xix).

Of course many things might be said in Freud's defence, such as, that he was a child of his time and not out of step with what was being said and done around him. Precisely! Is it a joke that Freud taught us to take jokes seriously, yet psychoanalysts might want to dismiss one of Freud's favourite jokes as just a joke? But if we do (or do not?) joke around with his joke, where might this lead us? Might it be read as telling us that psychoanalysis is a practice that is concerned with the foreign, that 'the negro' or foreigner is emblematic of the analysand, and psychoanalysis is a space for foreignness to make an appearance? But what is devouring in this case? Clearly the analyst feeds on the analysand, but is devour a revealing image? Is it different from one person 'feeding off' another in a conversation or dance? We may also ask, if the analyst is the lion and the analysand is 'the negro' about to be devoured, if we take this image seriously or play with it a bit, what is psychoanalysis? How can we begin to think about the power relations in the consulting room and on courses? Who is had for lunch and who makes it to the evening? Who manages to get on a training and to survive it?; who vanished without a trace? And can you be devoured slowly and imperceptibly, without your awareness of being absorbed into something?

This paper has focused on Freud. Something can be said about other psychoanalysts. Lavina Gomez writes,

> Klein's theoretical focus on the mother-child relationship and on the girl's development as a process in its own right redressed the male-centredness of Freudian theory. Her psychoanalysis does not otherwise address difference, rooted as it was in the social assumption which were reflected in current theory. The biological premises of psychoanalysis and the influence of Darwin's evolutionary theories meant that homosexual and lesbian development were inevitably seen as deviant; and because of the supposed universality

of psychoanalysis, little attention was paid to class, national or ethnic groupings ... Klein commented, however, that she would be very interested to analyse a person from a different culture, indicating that she thought there would be at least some important differences. She also remarked that she had found working with highly religious people difficult; the Freudian view of religion as illusion, which she shared, would have brought about a philosophical clash .... (Gomez, 1997, p. 50)

There is much of interest for us in this quotation. Here are just some of the issues. If Freud and Klein differ in what they say about female development, then what are we going to universalise here? If psychoanalysis is male-centred, then what are we doing when we seek to universalise it? Gomez claims that apart from addressing the girl's development, Klein does not otherwise address difference, as her thinking is rooted in the social assumptions of her time and place. There seems to be an acknowledgement that Klein did not analyse one person who was from a culture outside of Europe. It is worth remembering this, as is the comment that homosexual and lesbian development, as Gomez puts it, would be regarded as 'deviant' by Klein, and that she had found working with religious people difficult, because she shared the Freudian view of religion. Is this a picture of a cosmopolitan, urbane engagement with all people whatever their shape, size, shading, sexual preferences, their sense of the sacred and solemn? Or does it look embarrassingly narrow and likely to regard as foreign, strange, and a little ridiculous, if not deviant and dangerous, people who are not Europeans or heterosexual, and modernist enough to be hostile and critical to any way of seeing that is not modern science or psychoanalysis?

It is important to remember that it is not as if anyone who claims to be psychoanalytic and wants to insist on the universal application of psychoanalytic concepts has only Freud or Klein to choose between. Ferenczi and Rank were already moving psychoanalysis from a focus on the father and onto the centrality of the mother in 1925. They influenced psychoanalysis profoundly, and the direction of their work was later followed by Michael Balint and Donald Winnicott, for example. So do we have another three or four versions of what psychoanalysis is? So what are we applying when we make a claim for universally applicable? But of course the situation is much worse than this.

If there are over 500 types of Psychotherapy being practised today (David et al., 2018), it is likely that over 500 cases could be made for 'universal application'. Universal applicability might look very common and cheap. Many practitioners are tempted to claim that wherever they look they see support for the concepts they are most familiar with. Why would this surprise us?

We can consider the figure that Wittgenstein shows us in Philosophical Investigations, a figure that may be seen in one way by one person and as something else by another person, or as one way by one person then another by the same person. This is usually referred to as 'the duck-rabbit'. Following this, we might say that to be trained in psychoanalysis, for example, could be taken as being trained to see a rabbit and traces of rabbits. Others may be trained to see ducks. This does not mean that these others are wrong. Wittgenstein makes it difficult for us to duck the fact that the picture on the page does not alter and we do not need to refer to some representation of the image inside our mind changing to account for our going from only being able to see a rabbit to being able to see it as a duck. 'Seeing as' is about noticing an aspect, about seeing something as a beak or as ears, about putting something into a context. A training in psychoanalysis then may train us to see in the context of psychoanalysis, enabling us to gain citizenship of this state. Now, with our fellow citizens we see rabbits where it is possible to see a duck or a flying dolphin and perhaps many other ways. Those who fail to see rabbits may be dismissed as deviant, unenlightened or too stupid to see what is obvious. We may want to keep such people out of our organisation: to see and treat them as if they are 'foreigners', and not the nice 'foreigners' who want to integrate and assimilate, conforming to however we happen to live, but the 'foreigners' who have their own way of life and ways of seeing things, and fail to take it for granted that we must be right. If we can see a rabbit or rabbit like parts in each situation, we might say that what we have been trained to do is universally applicable because there are rabbits everywhere, so the concept of 'rabbit' applies everywhere. But perhaps we are only saying something about what we are most familiar with, what is habitual, what we are trained to do. What would it be like for you to look like a foreigner at psychoanalysis? Perhaps there is looking little a foreigner in psychoanalysis, as well as looking like a foreigner at psychoanalysis.

Looking like a foreigner

Writing about postmodernism, Loewenthal and Snell emphasise that they are interested in 'implication rather than application, in thoughtfulness rather than technique,' in how these ideas might help us to think, not in another school of psychotherapy or a technology for curing clients of what ails them (Loewenthal and Snell, 2003, p. 1).

In the 1930s Sandor Ferenczi was deeply concerned with the notion of expertise in psychoanalysis, with approaching psychoanalysis as if it is a technical and academic exercise, with the politics of power relations in the consulting room and in psychoanalysis. Ferenczi's argument with Freud is to do with Freud's wanting to think of psychoanalysis as something like a science, increasingly as something academic, whereas Ferenczi focuses more on the relationships between people, the politics of the consulting room, our not understanding, our needing to help to loosen the other person's tongue (Ferenczi 1933).

I am claiming that in the notion of a 'confusion of tongues', what is being evoked or appealed to is a meeting or a failure to meet between people from different cultures, who, therefore, speak different languages and cannot understand each other. I am also claiming that Ferenczi and Rank, by failing to agree and fall in with what was dominant in psychoanalysis at that time, were treated as if they were foreigners within psychoanalysis, and foreigners who kept their own ideas and identity, or rather, failed to integrate.

For Ferenczi, it might be said, the important thing is not our being in possession of universally applicable concepts but our willingness to try to engage and to be concerned about what might gets in the way of our engagement with others. The language of 'modernism' and 'postmodernism' would have been alien to him, but what is at stake here for me, and I think for him then, is not 'modernism' and 'postmodernism' but whether psychoanalysis is approached as a human technology, universally applicable to all people at all times in all places or, on the other hand, a cultural practice with the means for opening up conversations about how we experience and relate in and beyond the consulting room.

I am arguing that claims to universal validity are cheap, easy to make and made too often, but what is important about psychoanalysis is that it helps us to make sense not only of others but of ourselves in relation to others. Furthermore, the notion of the 'application' of psychoanalytic concepts gets us into issues to do with power, the potential violence of applying concepts to other human beings as if they are objects and we are subjects.

I would like to move us away from the 'application' of concepts to people in the way that a plasterer or bricklayer may apply what he has already prepared, perhaps slapping it on too thickly, and covering up what we cover. For, with people and many situations, subtleties and details need careful attention, and we often need something more like a gentle dab with a small brush after much squinting and hesitating. The language of 'application' speaks the languages of technology. What is valuable in psychoanalysis, I argue, is less this totalising tendency to see itself as explaining everything, but its opening of spaces for languages of emotional experience.

In Robert Rodman introduction to Winnicott and Rodman's (1999), The Spontaneous Gesture, he tells us that according to Klein and Joan Riviere, Winnicott, was not really making an original contribution to psychoanalysis, only providing evidence of his pathology, his 'block'. For he could not see that Klein said all the things he accused her of not saying (p. XX1). Here is another example, if we need another one, of psychoanalysts trying to shut down a space were difference and dialogue might appear by saying that those who look like foreigners are displaying their pathology. The idea here is that Klein's thinking forms a system that is applicable to all situations and not wanting to say what she says, not wanting to speak in this way, is an indication of hostility. Winnicott worried about psychoanalysis being presented as a system, in a dead language regarded as orthodox, true and universally applicable. He objected to dogma. Rodman writes, 'In objecting to dogma in the psychoanalytic endeavour, he is recommending obedience to the Second Commandment' (p. XXii). What are we to make of this remarkable claim?

I think Rodman says something profound and very important for our discussion of race, culture and difference generally. The Second Commandment is about not making and bowing down to 'graven images' of God. I understand Rodman as saying that a dogma in psychoanalysis is a graven image of our experience of living and we are always in danger of worshipping or fetishising. But in our devotion to the dogma, the actual experiences of people is at risk of falling out of the picture, and the dogma can be used to challenge and distort our experience.

This paper should make it clear that like Winnicott, I am worried about this tendency to think in terms of universal validity, about how dogmatic systems and party lines can crush people and their experiences. This is an anxiety about the tendency to try to conquer and dominate with theories and ideas rather than look again at what is in front of us.

I have emphasised the importance of looking like a foreigner rather than a conqueror at what happens around us, at others and at ourself, and I have argued against our being too interested in categories and concepts rather than our experience of living and what makes life worth living.

Disclosure statement

No potential conflict of interest was reported by the author(s).

References

Bracken, P., & Thomas, P. (2005). *Postpsychiatry: Mental health in a postmodern world*. oxford University Press.

Cushman, P. (2015). Relational psychoanalysis as political resistance. *Contemporary Psychoanalysis*, 51(3), 423–459. https://doi.org/10.1080/00107530.2015.1056076

David, D., Lynn, S. J., & Montgomery, G. H. (2018). *Evidence-based Psychotherapy*. The State of the Science and Practice, Wiley-Blackwell.

Derrida, J., & Dufourmantelle, A. (2000). *Of hospitality*. Stanford University Press.

Ferenczi, S. (1933). Confusion of tongues between adults and the child (The language of tenderness and of passion). In J. Borossa (Ed.), *Selected writings: SandorFerenczi* (pp. 293–303). Penguin.

Freud, S. (1930). Civilization and its discontents. In P. Gay (Ed.), *The Freud Reader, 1995* (pp. 722–772). Vintage.

Gomez, L. (1997). *An Introduction to Object Relations*. Free Association Books.

Kristeva, J. (1991). *Strangers to Ourselves*. Columbia University Press.

Levinas, E. (1969). *Totality and infinity: An essay on exteriority*. Duquesne University Press.

Levinas, E., & Kearney, R. (1984). *Dialogues with contemporary continental thinkers*. Manchester University Press.

Loewenthal and Snell. (2003). *Post-modernism for psychotherapists: A critical reader*. Brunner-Routledge.

Loewenthal, D. (2011). *Towards a therapy without foundations*. Taylor and Francis.

Lowe, F. (2013). *Thinking space: Promoting thinking about race, culture and diversity in psychotherapy and beyond*. Karnac Books.

Orbach, S. (2007). Democratizing Psychoanalysis. *European Journal of Psychotherapy and Counselling, March, 2007*(9910), 7–21. https://doi.org/10.1080/13642530601164455

Parker, I. (1999). *Deconstructing Psychotherapy*. Sage.

Parker, I. 2012. Foreword to Maher MJ, 2012. *Racism and cultural diversity*. karnac Books.

Phillips, A. (1997). *Terrors and experts*. Faber and Faber.

Rayner, E. (1994). *The independent mind in british psychoanalysis*. Free Association Books.

Stern, D. B., & Hirsch, I. (2017). *The interpersonal perspective in psychoanalysis, 1960s-1990s*. Routledge.

Szasz, T. (2006). What is psychoanalysis? In *Anne Casement edited Who owns psychoanalysis?* (pp. 25–39). Karnac.

West, D. (1996). *An introduction to continental philosophy*. Polity Press.

Winnicott, D., & Rodman, R. (1999). *The spontaneous gesture: Selected letters of D. W. Winnicott*. Karnac.

Language as Gesture in Merleau-Ponty: Some implications for method in therapeutic practice and research

Julia Cayne

ABSTRACT
The unexpected invention of a game with my grandchildren provided a new way of thinking about the nature of such unpredictable moments in therapy. The experience brought together a number of ideas, considered through the view of language taken by Merleau-Ponty where the chaotic primitive layers that pervade language are seen as having primacy over the rules of linguistics such as those set out by Saussure. Saussure is seen as providing a way of understanding linguistic structure whilst at the same time opening a number of ambiguities that then allow a way for thinking about language differently through Merleau-Ponty's emphasis on the usage of language (la parole) as opposed the structural aspects of language (la langue). Initially, Winnicott's ideas around the 'spontaneous gesture' are utilised to help show how this kind of unpredictable expression appears as something alive. Merleau-Ponty then shows how language as gestural phenomena takes hold of us through our bodies. Further questions then arise about the method in therapeutic practice and research. Here, it is argued that when the method is given primacy over experience, we are in a position that seeks the already known, which will not, therefore, permit some new expression to break through.

Introduction

So often experiences present us with new ways of thinking that seem to arise in us in ways that surprise and yet cannot be immediately understood. Suddenly we begin to be able to use words in unusual ways, to string them together in a new order. This can perhaps be seen in Shakespeare's writing where strings of his words have become phrases in common usage, for example, I have always been captivated by the phrase 'through a glass darkly'. Here something beyond the literal words is being hinted at. In this paper, there is an attempt to think about how we can suddenly use language in new ways. However, what is meant by 'new' is more to do with what was previously unthought-of by the individual rather than some universal 'new' which is not to say that others cannot also make sense of such an idea.

An experience of play with my grandchildren is first described and how this led to several ideas coming together in a way new to me, that also revealed something previously unrecognised about language. It is, however, difficult to convey how such an experience enables one to momentarily catch multiple ideas simultaneously. Secondly, Winnicott's (1987) notion of the 'spontaneous gesture' helped in thinking further about how something alive can seem to just happen and how we respond as therapists to such gestures seems to either allow our practice to come to life or impose something deadening. What then occurred was the reminder of language as having the potentiality for some kind of gestural impact beyond what is being said. Thirdly, the approach taken by Saussure (1983) is outlined as his is generally considered to be the originator of structural linguistics (his course on linguistics was initially published in 1916) providing a new way to think of language in terms of linguistic structure. However, the very differentiation he made between elements of the sign in his structural linguistics opened up a possibility for recognition of inherent difficulties in his ideas furthering new ways of understanding language. Fourthly, Merleau Ponty's (1962, 1973) view of language is seen to both anticipate (in the 1946 publication of Phenomenology of Perception) then engage with his discovery of Saussure's writing during the '40s and '50s, finally furthering his own thought in the later writing of the posthumously published 'The Visible and the Invisible' (1968) (It is worth noting that the publication dates/reprints do not reflect the order of the work). His rethinking of the structural aspects of language in terms of *'la langue'* and *'la parole'* emphasises the latter where the act of speech does not rest on a pre-existing set of linguistic rules (although these are not totally relinquished). It is this fluidity in the way we use language that seems to me to provide the possibility for something 'new' where language use becomes viewed as gestural, being a creative act that can suddenly, for example, reveal a new syntax as in the example of Shakespeare above. Fifthly consideration is given to some implications of these ideas for a method where approaches to qualitative phenomenological research, which set out a method, are still seen as stemming from the dominant discourse around a positivist paradigm. Such methods are viewed as positivist here, in that they can be seen to attempt to manoeuvre us around experience rather than recognise how we are subject to, in this case, language and importantly language as bodily phenomena. As such primacy is still given to universal truths rather than the contextual, temporal, cultural nature of being where it is argued what is most particular has the most possibility for meaning to others. Thus, there is a question of how we can research being from a more hermeneutic position where the method is recognised as the very approach that runs counter to phenomenology, in particular of Merleau Ponty. Reverie is proposed as phenomenological, being concerned with our bodily experience, whilst resisting being turned into a method.

The story and the gesture

One afternoon my grandchildren were drawing tiny figures and then cutting them out and laying them on the table. A draught caught them and a few fluttered around. Someone then blew one from their hand, someone else stuck one on their nose, someone else stuck one on their nose and blew it in the air. Then, chaos as everyone stuck these little figures on their nose and blew to see who's went furthest, someone yelled 'flying feathers'! It is of little importance who said what, what is important is that a moment of chance led to gesture after gesture, or what Winnicott (1971) might have called an invitation to play. There was a sense of connectedness without intrusiveness and feelings such as joy and competitiveness were just permitted. The idea of one person making a gesture to another, spontaneously, where the other person is able to play along took hold and almost at the same moment wondering how when we speak to each other we might be considered to be doing the same thing.

It would be useful here to outline the notion of the 'spontaneous gesture' (Winnicott, 1987) which is more a thread running through the letters in this book rather than a defined idea. However, spontaneity throughout his writings is connected with ways in which children, and adults, are able to express themselves conveying a sense of aliveness, being linked with creativity. A lack of such spontaneity would be seen to be a kind of deadness, which he linked, with the idea of the inauthentic 'false self' (Winnicott, 1989). However, what is mainly of interest in this paper is the idea that a gesture could be seen as a communication of an invitation to play, to another person, in a spontaneous moment. However, the way the other responds to such gestures can itself be deadening especially when the response is experienced as intrusive, what perhaps is needed is another spontaneous gesture. Stern (2004) also writes of such unpredictable, intersubjective moments as leading to therapeutic change. Laing sums up this kind of spontaneous occurrence rather beautifully by pointing out how really crucial moments in practice are 'unpredictable, unique, unforgettable, always unrepeatable and often indescribable' (Laing, 1967, p. 34). However, in Winnicott's thought the idea of a gesture can mostly be seen as play in the sense of some kind of bodily expression, as described above, whereas here there is a suggestion that we also play with language and such expression is also of the body.

Language and Saussure

The structuralist approach to language (which could be seen to originate in the work of Saussure (1983)) is explored here as a counterpoint to Merleau Ponty's (1973) gestural theory of language. Saussure's theory of linguistics focuses on the linguistic structure as different to language which he saw as involving various aspects including auditory and vocal, being social and also individual, having societal conventions, but having no discernible unity beyond the conventions. Language is seen here as a system of signs defined by their differentiation from other signs, and understanding this system is the work of linguistics. What Saussure then does is to take the sign and propose that it is made up of a sound pattern and an idea or concept of something, which he termed the signifier (which stands in for something else) and the signified (our concept of the thing or idea) respectively. The relationship between them is seen by Saussure as being arbitrary, by which he does not mean that personal choice is involved, and mostly there is no inherent link between the two. This seems to reveal a contradiction. On the one hand, he seems to be saying that we are bound by the linguistic community we inhabit, being unable to change a sign once it is in use, which seems to imply that structural linguistics views language as a stable system.

Sarup (1993) however points out that such stable structures indicate the view that, as subjects, we are independent, for example, of language. On the other hand, the concept and the sound pattern are not fixed to each other being arbitrary which opens up the possibility of something unstable at play that perhaps leads to ideas that are more concerned which how we may be subject to language.

It is this very instability that others then draw upon and so Saussure, whilst viewed as a structuralist also then paves the way for post-structuralism . For example, Lacan (1977) saw the signifier as having primacy over the signified in that it is the signifier that gives meaning but as the signified slides underneath, the signifier is said to signify other signifiers. Thus, meaning is always on the way and one can never be sure what a speaker's chain of signifiers will mean. In this sense, there is no final meaning. The last word of a sentence may convey what is meant but it can always be added to, changing what went before. Similarly, Merleau Ponty (1962) who is concerned with meaning sees the speaking subject as transforming the system which is not in any case viewed as a ready-made or stable system. Further language possesses us and not the other way round, but what does this mean?

Language: From structural theory to gestural phenomena

Schmidt (1985) considered whether Merleau-Ponty misread Saussure but it is difficult to be clear about this as Saussure, whilst seeking a systematised view of language, also opens up the possibility of seeing language as essentially unstable. Merleau-Ponty's thought on language emerges through his readings of Saussure but he believed he anticipated Saussure and then both acknowledges and diverges from structural linguistics (Schmidt, 1985). However, the divergence is already anticipated from the publication of The Phenomenology of Perception (1962) when his work is generally considered to be moving towards a concern with language and the body. There is an inherent problem in the writing of the body in that it could be seen to appear to give primacy to body over mind because of the cultural/historical way it has been used in opposition to mind. What body means in this paper, is related to the way Merleau-Ponty uses it as indicating but not reducible to mind, body and soul. This is perhaps part of the reason why Merleau-Ponty moved to the writing of 'flesh of the world' (1968).

There has also been a suggestion that those within the movement of structural linguistics, who saw Merleau-Ponty as misreading Saussure, did not themselves recognise the ambiguity within his thought Andén (2018). It is some of these ambiguities that are further considered here. One further point is that on reading Merleau-Ponty's thought on the language it seems more like an intertwining of one person's ideas with another, with points of convergence and divergence. Much like the project of 'The Visible and

Invisible' (1968), as concerned with seeing and being seen, touching and being touched, one could say that there is a similar intertwining occurring between Merleau-Ponty and Saussure, where the one is changed by the other.

Some interrelated ambiguities that Merleau-Ponty seems to pick up on in developing his view of language to be considered here are: Firstly his emphasis on the relationship between *'la langue'* and *'la parole'* and the way language use is viewed as a bodily expression where the gesture emerges through our relationship to the world and others. There is both recognition of the interplay between the diachronic or historical development of language and the synchronic or current usage of language, for Merleau-Ponty it seems that language is not a complete system at any given moment. Rather, the speaking subject transforms the system and the very structure of language can shift. Secondly, in the relationship between thought and speech, speech is seen as accomplishing thought rather than the other way around, hence why language has us and not we who have language. However, this relates to the question of the arbitrariness of the relationship between signifier and signified.

In Saussure (1983) the relationship between *'la langue'* and *'la parole'* makes a distinction between the structural aspects of language (*la langue*) and speech or the usage of language (*la parole*). Merleau Ponty (1973), however, seems to give primacy to the latter arguing that the structure of language rests on the use of language. Whilst language use and language structure are not reducible to the signifier and the signified they are related in that the sound pattern of the former involves the way the sign arrives to us, and then through us becoming an expression of the body. In other words, it is our experience with language that constructs language rather than purely some set of 'a priori rules, the spoken word is a genuine gesture, and it contains its meaning in the same way as a gesture contains its' (Merleau Ponty, 1962, p. 183). There are two aspects here both related to meaning, which it could be said is his main project, the nature of a gesture as a bodily expression and the gesture as pointing towards something.

The notion of the sign as a gesture stems from the idea that speech does not represent thought, we inhabit language and language pervades us. Speech is propelled through our body, a process ending with words. All this is related to the way the child comes to language and, unlike Saussure, Merleau-Ponty (1973) stresses the importance of how language develops through processes, initially of babbling and later of imitation that have a musical quality (p. 11). Thus, language acquisition is through a melodic response that he has previously anticipated as becoming the way language is *'singing the world'* expressing an *'emotional essence'* (1962, p. 187). The use of the term 'emotional essence' here seems to mean something of the way language can directly communicate emotion, perhaps more in the poetic sense that through the spoken word. Language as gesture also has a directional aspect, or rather points towards something. These two aspects then reveal something of our relationship to the world and in a sense disclose how it is not so much that we are in the world but rather we are of the world. As such, gestural language could be seen as expression through the body resonating with the resonances within which we are bathed. Thus, when we speak we reveal something of our own position in the world where the body already grasps what is happening prior to any sense being made or conceptualisation. Hence, we are led by how the world calls to us, our body already takes up a place from which to view that which we have turned our attention towards.

Whilst vocabulary and syntax appear to have a set of rules, and as such, are known to us, speech is not viewed as a representation of thought but something transformative. The idea of language as gestural expressions of the body (no distinction of mind and body is made here) hints at something primal at play that will not be known by attempting to understand such a gesture. For example, of anger he says:

> I do not see anger or a threatening attitude as a psychic fact hidden behind the gesture, I read anger in it. The gesture does not make me think of anger, it is anger in itself.. (Merleau Ponty, 1962, p. 184)

Also,

> I do not understand the gesture of others by some act of intellectual interpretation; communication between consciousnesses is not based on the common meaning of their respective experiences, for it is equally the basis of that meaning. The act by which I lend myself to the spectacle must be recognised as irreducible to anything else. Merleau Ponty, 1962, p. 185.

Here speech, as the usage of language, expresses meaning not in a sense of representing or containing the meaning but rather as conveying the place we take up in the world. Thus, understanding what others say to us comes to us through the body in much the way that music can communicate with us. Furthermore, if language is infused with this kind of primordial, musical quality we cannot know our or others' experience through any intellectual activity. We need to listen to our bodily responses. All this raises vital questions about how we speak and are spoken to in psychotherapeutic practice and research and how much is missed by a method which by its nature attempts to bring to bear a pre-determined set of criteria on experience. Raising questions about the intellectual interpretation or working out is not intended as an anti-theoretical position in terms of practice or research or indeed to suggest that Merleau Ponty did. Rather through consideration of the relationship between language and the body, theoretical ideas like other ideas could be seen to come to us through the body, as opposed to an intellectual application, and as such are connected to this idea of the 'speaking word'. It is thus argued that as such when we embody an idea it communicates in the way of the gesture to the other person. Thus, we may have intellectual knowledge prior to a situation but there are times and ways when it comes to us anew.

It seems so much easier, when listening to music, to allow the music to call to us, we do not generally try to explain what is being communicated so much as we allow it to take hold of us. Dreyfus (2014) argues that Merleau-Ponty is unique in recognising that we are led by the object calling on our body and when we perceive something our body leads us to the optimum distance to view. Further, it is not rules, criteria and concepts that guide us but the body that grasps what is happening and if anything we have learned not to heed this. True gestures are not about objectively representing things but are rather expressions of emotional essence. Their meaning is not even revealed at the last word, with meaning lying hitherto what Merleau-Ponty (1962) called: ' ... the elaboration of scientifically conceived objects'. Further, 'I do not understand the gestures of others by some act of intellectual interpretation' (p. 185).

Finally, it is in his view of that aspect of language called *'parole'* where Merleau-Ponty can be seen to depart from Saussure, something already anticipated in the Phenomenology of Perception (1962, pp. 184–197). Not all speech is seen as gestural, a gesture is something that 'breaks the primordial silence'. There is an ambiguity within *'parole'* that recognises the difference between *'a speaking word'* and *'a spoken word'*. What this seems to mean is that in the former something breaks through what might be considered to be the ready-made meanings of the latter, something of our being, that was previously unformulated, comes into existence. This is what is meant here by the idea of something new. Furthermore, this gesture conveys something emotional where something of our being is gaining expression; thus, the link between the signified and the signifier can no longer be considered to be always arbitrary.

Between body and method

If we understand language in the ways outlined here, in particular, the ideas around the body as of the world, or rather what Merleau Ponty (1968) later terms *flesh of the world*, then what are the implications for the ways we approach to practice and research (the terms are used interchangeably here)? What is needed in understanding the gestures of others cannot be set out as a system of pre-determined rules (method) but is defined by what is not required or what is experienced through our bodies. He argues as follows:

> Communication between consciousnesses is not based on the common meaning of their respective experiences, for it is equally the basis of that meaning. The act by which I lend myself to the spectacle must be recognised as irreducible to anything else. I join it in a kind of blind recognition which precedes the intellectual working out and clarification of the meaning. (Merleau Ponty, 1962, p. 185)

Further, this *'blind recognition'* comes to us through our collusion with the world and our intermingling with others. Elsewhere, I have written about how this kind of engagement is fraught with disorientation and uncertainty and as a result, one could see the creation of phenomenological methods as an attempt to orientate ourselves (Cayne, 2014). Such need for orientation leads to various forms of positivism whether the objectivity of measurement or the merger inherent in pure subjectivism. It seems such a logical idea that having a clear method will also help situate us in our research, but what is lost by positioning ourselves, through a method, is our own position in the world where we might be more able to hear what is calling to us. It is argued here that method intervenes between our body and the world and further manoeuvres our body as opposed to permitting our bodily reaction to attune us to what calls to us. The problem with being positioned is that we are taken to the reassurance of the domain of the already known tending to give primacy to the method rather than our experience, which will hinder the emergence of something new.

Phenomenology is more concerned with possibility than probability (as concerned with the mathematical likelihood of an event being due to chance). It is not the intention here to argue against all kinds of positivist research. Rather, it is to argue against the reduction of phenomenology to the method by drawing on positivist criteria to validate what is essentially a different domain being concerned with experience and meaning. For example, in undertaking previous research on learning about the unknown (Cayne, 2004) I found a number of difficulties with the phenomenological method. Most phenomenological methods require texts such as interview transcripts to be broken down for analysis which in Giorgi's (1985) method are called meaning units. The need to do this appears to stem from the premise 'Since one cannot analyze a whole text simultaneously, one has to break it down into manageable units' (Giorgi, 1985, p. 11). Such an exercise is quite different from Merleau Ponty's (1968) view as follows:

> The meaning is not on the phrase like the butter on the bread, like a second layer of "psychic reality" spread over sound: it is the totality of what is said, the integral of all the differentiations of the verbal chain; it is given with the words for those who have ears. (p. 155)

What I found was that in analysing units of meaning something was lost which was only noticed on a second analysis (drawing on ideas about reverie) of the interview texts where I listened to the tape recordings and allowed my own bodily reactions, including thoughts, to come to me. Such an approach is quite different from attending to experience through the method and this is where the difference between *'a speaking word'* and *'a spoken word'* became most noticeable. I began to notice much more of what was happening between myself and the interviewees with intersubjective experiences such as power at play, anxiety, people I felt connected to and those I did not, how some people wanted to tell their stories and some wanted to conceal theirs. In summary, I experienced moments of aliveness but also moments of deadness about which I was able to begin to wonder. Additionally, I realised that in telling their story the other tells you how to listen. People said things like: 'learning occurs in a relationship where the other is willing to learn too', how the experience of learning 'comes from throw away remarks and not over prepared lessons' and for another 'life and living is the teacher'. These ideas highlight how the researcher needs to live with what is said and be willing to learn anew understanding that we change and are changed by what we research. The experience tells us how to look as well as what to look at whereas the use of the method hindered my ability to hear a *'speaking word'*.

Phenomenology is concerned with meaning and the meanings we ascribe to our experience. However, for Merleau Ponty (1968), meaning emerges in the between of intersubjectivity. As such, the meaning is not already located, being horizontal, and the gestural aspects of language mean that the expression is creative rather than representational. The problem is that if we change and are changed by what we explore then validity and reliability as meant in a positivist sense (i.e. as accurately reflecting the data with consistency in the use of the methods of analysis, respectively) are problematic. Even Lincoln and Guba (1985) oft-cited requirements for rigour within qualitative research, based on truth value, applicability, consistency, and neutrality could be seen as positivist in the sense that here again are criteria for deciding the value of what might be discovered. Language as gesture calls for the therapist/researcher to lend oneself to the spectacle, which might mean something like listening with one's body, being open to being changed and reinventing our approach as the situation demands of us. In revealing such processes we might also reveal the value of even a single moment in terms of what has the possibility for others. Possibility, for example, in Kierkegaard (1985, 1992) is concerned with what might bring something alive and new, breaking through rigidities such as what has become a dominant scientific discourse which can leave us in despair.

The possibility of reverie came closer, for me, to not putting method first. Ideas within Bachelard's (1971) notion of reverie helped me to break through the method so that I could hear others and myself in new ways. It is suggested here that reverie is a phenomenological way forward for those for whom it seems to have the possibility, but not by being turned into another method. In some ways revere resists such usage being concerned with what not to do (negative capability) and not being able to predict what thoughts will come to one and how that will happen. Reverie was phenomenological for Bachelard with its concern with imagination, dreaming and the poetic, not concerned with representing but accomplishing a creative act. If 'the poetic image places us at the origin of the speaking being' (Bachelard, 1994, p. xxiii) then reverie could be seen to be the state of being that allows us to be stirred.

> Through this reverberation, by going immediately beyond all psychology or psychoanalysis, we feel poetic power rising naively within us. After the original reverberation, we are able to experience resonances, sentimental repercussions, reminders of our past. But the image has touched the depths before it stirs the surface. And this is true of a simple experience of reading. The image offered us by reading the poem now becomes really our own. It takes root in us. It has been given by another, but we begin to have the impression we created it. It becomes a new being in our language, expressing us by making us what it expresses; in other words, it is at once a becoming of expression, and a becoming of our being. Here expression creates being."(Bachelard, 1994, p. xxiii)

Others such as Bion (e.g. 1970) and Ogden (1997) write of reverie and the way it opens up creative ways of attending to thoughts and images that frequently don't at first seem to make sense to us. However, Bachelard's approach is more clearly concerned with poetic imagination and the body through the idea of engaging with the emotional/sensual, through phenomenology. Further, whilst reverie was considered by Bachelard to be phenomenological, its nature as what might be called the non-intentional, means that such an approach resists positing, being concerned with words that dream.

Conclusions

The view of language as gestural phenomena arising and expressed through the body in relation to the world reveals us as of the world. Such gestures indicate something alive, although may also reveal something deadening too, and creative at play. If we wish to permit the possibility of something new emerging we need to become involved, prior to any understanding, being able to move freely with the instability of language or perhaps to make free with the language. How we respond to others also comes to us through our body, which already finds the place from which to attend, whereas method will manoeuvre us differently ensuring we see through the glass that has its focus attuned to what is already known.

Merleau-Ponty's phenomenology with its emphasis on language as a bodily phenomenon has the possibility of shaking us from well-worn paths that hinder the emergence of the unexpected of being, and a key theme of this paper is an emerging question of how we might learn anew. Here there is the beginning of an attempt to re-engage with questions of how we might conceal being through the method, (or perhaps more how we restrict something new breaking through) which is difficult enough if we are claiming that phenomenology is our guide. It could be argued, however, that there is a difference between engaging with practice and research phenomenologically (and it seems to me to be worth pursuing what this means especially given the differences within the phenomenological tradition) rather than through phenomenological methods which, have emerged mostly through a discourse associated with the positivist tradition. Thus, the proposal here is a return to engaging with phenomenology, which is a rather different guide in the methodological sense, prior to what may be seen as the additional layer of the method.

Disclosure statement

No potential conflict of interest was reported by the author(s).

References

Andén, L. (2018). Language and tradition in Merleau-Ponty's reading of Husserl and Saussure. *Studia Phaenomenologica, XV111*, 183–205. https://doi.org/10.5840/studphaen2018189
Bachelard, G. (1971). *The poetics of reverie*. Beacon Press.
Bachelard, G. (1994). *The poetics of space*. Beacon Press.
Cayne, J. (2004). *Developing a methodology exploring the unknown in the acquisition of psychotherapeutic knowledge* [Unpublished PhD]. University of Surrey
Cayne, J. (2014). Disorientation and wild delusion. *Self and Society, 41*(3), 3. https://doi.org/10.1080/03060497.2014.11084364
Dreyfus, H. (2014). *Skillful coping: Essays on the phenomenology of everyday perception and action*. Oxford University Press.
Giorgi, A. (1985). Sketch of a Psychological Phenomenological Method. In A. Giorgi (Ed.) *Phenomenology and Psychological Research*. Pittsburgh: Duquesne University Press.
Kierkegaard, S. (1985). *Fear and trembling*. Penguin.
Kierkegaard, S. (1992). *Concluding unscientific postscript to philosophical fragments*. Princeton University Press.
Lacan, J. (1977). *Ecrits*. Routledge.
Laing, R. D. (1967). *The politics of experience*. Pantheon Books.
Lincoln, Y., & Guba, E. (1985). *Naturalistic inquiry*. Sage.
Merleau Ponty, M. (1962). *The phenomenology of perception*. Routledge.
Merleau Ponty, M. (1968). *The visible and the invisible*. Northwestern University Press.

Merleau Ponty, M. (1973). *Consciousness and the acquisition of language.* Northwestern University Press.
Sarup, M. (1993). *An introductory guide to pos- structuralism and postmodernism.* Harvester Wheatsheaf.
Saussure, D. F. (1983). *Course in general linguistics.* Duckworth.
Schmidt, J. (1985). *Maurice Merleau-Ponty. Between phenomenology and structuralism.* McMillan.
Stern, H. W. (2004). *The present moment in psychotherapy and everyday life.* W. W. Norton & Co.
Winnicott, D. W. (1971). *Playing and reality.* Routledge.
Winnicott, D. W. (1987). *The spontaneous gesture.* London: Karnac.
Winnicott, D. W. (1989). *Holding and interpretation.* London: Karnac.

The private life of meaning - some implications for psychotherapy and psychotherapeutic research

Tony McSherry, Del Loewenthal and Julia Cayne

ABSTRACT
This article outlines differences between phenomenology and method, with implications for psychotherapy and psychotherapeutic research. Drawing on a study exploring how mental health nurses are therapeutic, we focus on how taking experience seriously is encouraged through being phenomenological. We look at how research method and theory – and fixed beliefs or ideas – tend to constrict language, so that personal (sensual) meaning is lost or curtailed. Being phenomenological instead 'opens up' language and consequently meaning, in an act of truthfulness through speaking one's experience, which we see as both psychotherapeutic and a valid form of research.

Introduction

In this article, we draw on a study that explored learning and the therapeutic in mental health nursing practise, through interviews with 10 mental health nurses working in community and in-patient settings (McSherry, 2018). Two approaches to research were followed in this study, one employing Giorgi's (2002, 2006, 2009) established empirical phenomenological method, and the other based on some aspects of Husserl (1927/1971; 1952/1989; 1960; /1962/1977; 1969; 1970a, 1970b; 1973; 1982), Heidegger's (1930, 1962, 1985) and Merleau-Ponty (1945/2014; 1964; 1968) writings on phenomenology. Key illustrative aspects of the method and findings from the empirical study, based on Giorgi's approach (Giorgi, 2009), will be outlined, after which our intention is to address questions on method and truthfulness which arose from the second phenomenological approach.

Our aim is to show something of how we get 'caught up' in method, or theory, and this 'captivity' or entanglement closes off wider experience. While we are referring often to 'method' as empirical research method, we also intend it to include any theory, idea, belief, dogma, or way of relating, that constricts language. We hope this will be clear to the reader. We intend to show that being phenomenological involves opening up to experience again. Our view is that the language of a research method imposes a constriction on the way findings can be found so that the findings are not recognised as valid findings as such unless they are subsumed into the language of that method. We are not saying that phenomenologists are not also caught up in this, but we believe that in being phenomenological we are less likely to become so. As we will try to show, the constricting of language has crucial significance especially in the field of meaning.

The constriction of meaning we will call 'given' meanings, in that the words used have been removed from their contextual origin or 'sensual' meaning. We will try to demonstrate this difference firstly in outlining the origin of the study, and then follow with its importance for research and psychotherapy involving meaning generally.

Origins of the study – experiences of mental health nursing

This study is rooted in two areas of experience personal to the main researcher. The first is linked to taking seriously one's experience. This is linked to how the main researcher had tried to transpose a former way of living as a Franciscan friar in a religious community onto working in mental health nursing, not realising that we cannot separate meaning from context. As Husserl would put it, our experience of truth must not be 'torn ... from ... [the] context of subjective mental living' (Husserl, 1969, §59 in Welton, 1999, p. 262). Husserl's emphasis in his phenomenology on staying with experience consequently emerged as fundamentally important, as it was the 'tearing' of the meaning of being a Franciscan friar (the Franciscans are a Christian religious order) and 'translating' it into the work of being a mental health nurse, that gave rise to a feeling of abjection for the main researcher, long before this study had been thought of. This feeling, at first, had no 'truthful' way of being understood as it was difficult to trust experience. At first, such distress was theorised in terms of the psychoanalytic notion of abjection – something to do with, and left to, the feminine, of disgust, excluded from patriarchal reason (Kristeva, 1982) – and it seemed that mental health nursing itself was an abject discipline (McSherry et al., 2015). For some time, this abject feeling had a 'fixed', or static' sense, until a certain realisation began through speaking with others. What will become clear is that it is the context of meaning that is vital here that what brings the meaning of experience alive (what we call the 'sensual' aspect) is related to a subjective, personal, and private context. Through the course of this study, it was only with time and through others that the main researcher's experience could be spoken of in a certain truthfulness, understanding the feeling of abjection through being attentive, rather than dismissing it as a kind of an inability to cope with the difficulties of the psychiatric setting (for example). Wittgenstein's note from his personal notebooks seems especially apposite here:

'One *cannot* speak the truth; if one has not yet conquered oneself. One *cannot* speak it – but not, because one is not yet clever enough' (Wittgenstein, 1998, p. 41 in Heaton, 2010, p. 32)

The second personal experience which gave rise to this study was noticing that only some mental health nurses appeared to be therapeutic in their way of being with patients. Those therapeutic nurses appeared to have an attitude that involved something other than implementing the psychiatric treatment of medication as cure, the biomedical model of mental illness that dominates mental health nursing (see, for example, Gray et al., 2010; Jones, 2009). Cutcliffe (2000) contrasts this dominant attitude in mental health nursing with another attitude involving an art to healing which involves a personal process. Although the two attitudes are not necessarily mutually exclusive, it is this latter attitude, involving the therapeutic as the art of healing which was the focus of this research.

Informally observing colleagues in the mental health nursing milieu, speaking with and being with another seemed to be about an openness to the other person. Speaking is linked to an oral tradition, in which speech involves a whole, embodied experience (Heaton, 2010). Therapeutic mental health nurses speaking with others seemed to involve a certain search for 'truthfulness', but in an embodied way rather than following theoretical arguments or ideas. Ways of being therapeutic in this encounter were explored in terms of tacit knowledge, emotional labour, intuition and openness. These informal observations of everyday practise were reflected in aspects of the literature in nursing indicating that therapeutic mental health nurses spent time speaking with, and being with, others who were in mental distress (Eriksen, Arman, Davidson, Sundfør & Karlsson, 2013; Eriksen et al., 2014). While this 'being with' may appear as intuitively obvious, mental health nurses in fact spend most of their time on administrative duties and administering medication (Zauszniewski et al., 2012). The latter situation is reflected in the empirical findings of our study; all participants were troubled by it; for example, one participant was convinced that 'risk management trumps all', and one found the lack of time with patients as 'soul destroying'. The findings from our study also show that the mental health nurses interviewed work therapeutically through being open, speaking with and being with patients in various ways, although in the service of psychiatry, and they have learned mainly from life experience and practice.

These two experiences gave rise to a question on what it was that mental health nurses felt they were doing that was therapeutic and how they had learned to be so. Giorgi's (2009) approach was chosen because it is an established research method, rooted in Husserl's philosophy. The study also indicated whether an empirical research method could throw light on what was happening in that embodied speaking between mental health nurses and patients. We will now outline Giorgi's research method, and highlight an important problem that we regard is relevant to the psychological therapies, and to psychotherapeutic research on meaning.

Giorgi's (2009) empirical phenomenological method

Giorgi (2009) developed his empirical phenomenological research method over many years, basing it on Husserl's descriptive phenomenology. Husserl aimed to elucidate the essential structure of consciousness in order to provide a foundation of all sciences (Heidegger, 1962/2008; Husserl, 1960; Zahavi, 2003). The only consciousness he had direct access to was his own, and so his project focused on what he could learn directly from his own consciousness.

Husserl believed that experience could be trusted as a source of valid knowledge, through being open to an 'originary giving intuition' (Zahavi, 2003, p. 45 – after §24 of Husserl's (1982) *Ideas I*), but that because of pervasive ideas of science we had lost touch with this trust. Husserl developed the idea of the reduction, from the Latin word for 'leading back'; this concept involves putting to one side all one's assumptions and previously held knowledge of a phenomenon in order to see it afresh, to 'lead back' it to its essence. Part of this process may also involve 'free imaginative variation', a process through which we remove characteristics from a concept until its meaning collapses so that consequently we notice what is essential to that phenomenon, what makes it what it is (Moran, 2000). Giorgi's (2009) phenomenological method, adapting Husserl's ideas to psychology, attempts to describe the essence, or essential structure, of a phenomenon, such as, for example, a mental health nurse's meaning regarding his/her experience of being therapeutic with patients.

A problem with method, through the example of Giorgi's method

In deference to the scientific psychological community which he serves, Giorgi developed his method to be repeatable, and testable, following set steps (Giorgi, 2009). Giorgi (2009) appeals to method in order to be able to present to the other's consciousness (the critical other as a community) a form of common language (a certain empirical language), so that 'what is going on in the researcher's consciousness' can be checked and critiqued by that community. By default, this constrains the language used. The most important step we see in his method consequently is the transformation of the words of the research participant into *transformed meaning units* of accepted psychological language. This transformation, or translation, we would regard, loses the phenomenological aspect of the experience of what is involved in trying to grasp the meaning of the participant's words. As a result, the 'sensual' context of the meaning has been lost and replaced by 'given' psychological meanings. What we mean by 'sensual' here is the personal, subjective context (or landscape) of the participant's meaning that he/she is trying to convey.

An example may show this. One participant in this study gauged being therapeutic in terms of how she would care for her father. The transformed meaning unit for her spoken words, that is, translated into psychological language, reads as: *'Treating a person like someone she loved is therapeutic'*. This 'given' language we can all understand, and we in the psychological scientific community can broadly empathise with her meaning through it. However, if we dispense with having to transform her words into psychological language and stay instead with the phenomenological experience of her spoken words, 'something else' comes through (some details have been altered or removed to protect confidentiality):

> When she touched on how she came into nursing, her speech was full of pauses, stops and starts, the beginnings of sentences taken up and then abandoned. It was unclear which way to go, yet this uncertainty itself seemed important. It opened a space between us that allowed silences to be. In this space she spoke about ... [...] ... her ... [...] father ... [...] ... There was an intense sense of sadness ... [...] ... Without knowing about it much, it seemed somewhere there was a regret for 'not being there' to a father ... There was an entangled grief here perhaps [the researcher's and the participant's grief].

We call this 'something else' the 'sensual' context of the words, which emanate from a memory that cannot be experienced fully and is perhaps entangled with the researcher's own memories. The reduction here can be seen to be the researcher's attempt to 'see', through a disentanglement, what it is in his consciousness that belongs to the participant in her response.

Giorgi (2002, 2006) notes that he is not at ease with his attempt to satisfy the wider scientific community, and still feels marginalised within that community. Respectfully, we suggest that it appears that Giorgi (2009) has become caught up in a meaning, one which his scientific community has imposed, or 'given' to him, that his findings must be 'scientific'. We would consider that this difficulty applies to all methods that attempt to constrict the language of meaning into a specialist language. Or in other words, to transpose a subjective, personal experience onto a given one. For example, returning to the origin of the study, 'caring for' someone from the reality of being a Franciscan is completely different to 'caring for' someone in the mental health nursing milieu (which is devoid of the Franciscan 'landscape of meaning').

What appears to offer a way out of such a constriction seems to be about trusting experience, our own embodied feeling about something, and allowing ourselves to be in relation to another (or others) thoughtful enough to invoke a genuine curiosity about ourselves and others, come what may. Crucial to this process is the opening up of language, and indeed speech, so that words and images that present themselves can be appreciated and noted rather than channelled into 'psychological language'. Seeing this constriction of language for what it is clearly took some time.

A phenomenological approach

It appears that what could not be shown through Giorgi's (2009) method was what was going on in the consciousness of the researcher, or what was 'felt' in the 'originary giving intuitions', through 'being with' each participant throughout each interview, and afterwards on listening, and thinking about each. We will try to illustrate this further here.

Through not following any method but allowing experience to be taken seriously – what we would call being phenomenological – what emerged was how being with people felt like being called into a relation, in which there was a freedom, or openness, which also puts us under question (as researchers, therapists, participants).

An example of a phenomenology of an interview is presented below (some details have been changed or removed to protect confidentiality):

> 'I'm grateful for you talking' was the line addressed to her, before any thoughts found their mark. It simply 'showed itself' that she needed to be appreciated. This impression may have been something to do with a surface confidence at times rippled by a certain tremor in her voice and how she closed her eyes momentarily as if not to see something. The meanings in the interview seemed to lap back on each other in time, so that later, talking about a patient, the sense of denial in how she said 'I don't expect ... any acknowledgement' confirmed the original impression. It seemed confusing as to which meanings belonged to whom ... [...] ... In the middle of the interview she spoke about her parents who were ... [...] ... un-interested and this seemed like a crystal ball in the dance hall to fling its colours indifferently onto every surface. Her aunt had rescued her by stepping in, and they would play 'charades', board games and read stories out loud together. She knew a lot about communication skills ... [...] ... [...] .... Experience of life had made her critical of empathy and psychiatry. But what seemed to throw its light into every shadow was how she closed her eyes sometimes as if to block out something, even though she said it was important 'to make some sort of bond and open up lines of communication'. What was therapeutic for her was the tactile, the sensory, the reassuring touch, that someone was present, and certain words, like thoughts perhaps as well, could be 'shelved'. She said she had learned about being therapeutic also through 'shadowing' her mentor. Her speech often shot across like stones skimming on a glassy surface. But when the throw was not so good, the glass broke and something foundered .... [With clients] ... she did not want to 'open a box of worms'. It seemed so accurate, speaking about her nurse training, when she said 'all this nonsense we learnt'. It seemed that ... [someone] ... had failed her, consigned her to the shadows ... [...] ... and what she needed was someone to help her step out of there ... [...] ...

The experience of trying to perceive in consciousness (the researcher's) what this participant is communicating is shot through with uncertainty, but perhaps allows something of the sensual landscape to emerge that informs this nurse in her everyday work. But the meanings cannot be fixed into a given certainty. Something could change if she were interviewed again, perhaps even the whole landscape. We are reminded of how Heidegger speaks of 'letting beings be' (*Gelassenheit*) (Heidegger, 1930, p. 129-130, in Polt, 1999, p. 127), that is, to show themselves through an evolving attentive involvement (Polt, 1999).

An excerpt from the same participant's synthesis from Giorgi's method seems instead like a list of 'facts':

> *Being therapeutic involves something of the self, acknowledging the other as an individual with unique characteristics, and encouraging the person to develop skills and competencies that have been stunted in childhood ... [...] ... Skills learned from training courses are helpful in engaging others in order to become therapeutic. One can care, as it is a formal approach, without being therapeutic ... . [...] ... Competencies are innate rather than learned or taught. Adverse childhood experiences have given her the competencies of resilience and being able to challenge others ... [...] ... University training did not encourage critical or original thinking ... [...] ...*

There is a translation of the participant's meanings into psychological language that we can comprehend, but the language is narrowed, leaving little room for uncertainty or what 'uncertainty' might mean.

Coming to learn and to be therapeutic

The uncertainty in the phenomenological text brings to mind Heidegger, 1962/2008, (pp. 192-195 [151-153]) hermeneutic circle, in which there is 'hidden a positive possibility of the most primordial kind of knowing'. The circle seems to remain open in the phenomenological account, while in the empirical account it seems already static. The phenomenological text also appears to show something of the person of the nurse, where she is coming from in her being to an extent, or what we have called 'sensual' meaning.

Through this process of attempting to stay with experience, it felt like a discovery to 'feel' the difference between what has been distinguished phenomenologically as sensual and given meaning, like finding a new discovery as if 'for the first time for oneself', and then noticing later on that others had come this way before. In this case, for example, Husserl (1982) (Zahavi, 2003, p. 149) and Merleau-Ponty, (1945/2014; 1964; 1968) (Freeman, 1993; Shaw, 2014) came to notice these differences, as indeed did Freud, 1915/2001, (p. 214).

Wittgenstein's (1998) distinction about being 'truthful' only if we have come by the way of our own 'truthfulness' (Heaton, 2010, p. 32) comes to life here, because it is through the effects of discovering for (and of) oneself that we begin to speak truthfully. This way of 'discovering' appears to have been more like a 'primordial kind of knowing' (Heidegger, 1962/2008, pp. 192-195 [151-153]) in a sensual landscape than a rational, deductive process, although it is not that reason and deduction are not important.

It appears that one's own truthfulness involves entering into, and taking seriously, one's own sensual landscape in which words are living things. Is this not perhaps what therapy and research are all about? – Coming to know and understand ourselves truthfully.

Fixed ways of being

However, what happens if this process of learning stalls? What happens if it sediments into a situation where beliefs never seem to change, but repeat inexorably, so a person (to put learning philosophically) may *not* be 'constantly compelled to face the possibility of disclosing an even more primordial and more universal horizon from which we may draw the answer to the question, "What is "Being"?"' (Heidegger, 1962/2008, § 49/26-27; see also Polt, 1999, p. 41). Openness to therapeutic learning seems to be blocked for some people (at least for a time), and is perhaps to do with being 'captivated' in something like a fixed meaning (Merleau-Ponty, 1945/2014, pp. 137/170). Similarly, we could think of this stalling of learning as a gestalt, where it seems as if a 'concept forces itself on one' (Wittgenstein, 2009, pp. 215, § 191). It seems that learning appears to involve a 'painful' openness to an 'other' person, in which we are called into question. But if a person is 'fixed' in his/her way of being, captivated by something, then it is likely that learning in terms of openness will be hampered. Therapeutic learning, and learning in research, in terms of openness may therefore come to an end when confronted by a fixed state of being, akin to adherence to a rigid dogma. A question that arises here is whether openness to learning therapeutically can be learned, or nurtured, only if it is already innate. Many of the participants in our study believed that being therapeutic was innate.

The uncertain relation to the other

It appears then that what it seems Husserl's phenomenology invokes is something quite simple, in that it encourages a way of speaking freely of what we perceive, privileging the 'giveness' of experience (Husserl, 1970a §51 in Welton, 1999, p. 21). Speech seems to be 'opened up' through taking seriously that ' ... the originary giving intuition ... [is] ... the source of all knowledge' (Zahavi, 2003, p. 45, after Husserl, 1982, §24). But this 'opening up' itself appears to be made possible through relating to someone who is already like this. In this respect, what appeared was that the 'other person' called into question one's own meanings, and then one's own attempts to understand these same meanings may be seen as impositions on that other person. It may be that this kind of relation is signalled, 'signposted', by simple statements in the interviews like 'she accepts me', or 'just keep being there'. These statements seem loaded with ambiguity, tacit understanding and feeling.

In what we consider as being phenomenological, it was apparent that the 'originary giving intuition' was a dream-like landscape (as illustrated by our examples), where there was a confusion about what imagery was important and what was not, and ultimately, it seemed that meaning that counted therapeutically was sensual (personal, contextual and private). A private landscape that is 'overrun with words' (Merleau-Ponty, 1968, p. 155). This kind of 'private life' of meaning seemed to indicate that we do not know each other, except through fragments of 'spoken' speech which seem to be pointers towards another personal landscape. When we are sure therefore that we have 'understood' the other, it may be worthwhile reminding ourselves of Husserl's view that at times empathy is a kind of 'self-alienation' (Husserl, 1970b, p. 189 in Zahavi, 2003, p. 124), and we have probably got our understanding of the other wrong. This is in contrast to empathy of the other given as a whole – he/she may be talking, laughing or dancing – so that I see him or her as an expressive unity (Zahavi, 2014 after Husserl, 1952).

Landscapes of meaning

Husserl's insistence that the 'originary giving intuition' (Zahavi, 2003, p. 45, after Husserl, 1982, §, p. 24) says something important about ourselves and reality, and Merleau-Ponty's (1968, p. 155) imagery of words 'overrunning' a landscape, seemed to say something here about language belonging in a 'truthfulness' of experience.

Being open phenomenologically to meaning in the relation in terms of 'me and this other person' opened up the senses of meaning as 'given' and 'sensual' through a creative process. Meanings easily become 'given', separated from the 'sensual' aspect, and there is no acknowledgement of the seriousness of the failure of the spoken word to 'accomplish' (Merleau-Ponty, 1964, p. 46) a meaning. Heidegger (1985, § 6, p. 56 in Moran, 2000, p. 234) perhaps sums this up in his observation that, 'We do not say what we see, but rather the reverse, we see what one says about the matter'. The 'given' of accepted meanings overwhelms the private 'sensual' meaning.

The 'meanings' of the words in a sensual landscape are like screeching wild birds, clamouring through the trees. But if those 'words' (sounds) are taken only in their 'given' meaning it is like removing the wild birds to a reserve, an aviary, in which they sit speechless and in mourning (the landscape to which they belong having been removed). This seems to be what the imposition of a theory, or idea, does to another person (however helpful that theory or idea may be at times) – it separates the meaning from the sensual landscape and the person is left in an alien world, alienated from himself or herself. Separation of the given meaning of a 'word' from its sensual (private and unfolding) meaning involves an alienating violence but appears to happen all the time. An example of this alienation might be imposing our theoretical ideas, or our 'evidence-based' ideas, on the other person in therapy, or in research.

The sensual landscape may also contain 'savage creatures' – it is not necessarily a 'nice' place but rather something that speaks in truthfulness. Reflecting the sensual, we appear to be linked to the other in a relation which is asymmetrical and uncertain in terms of trying to define, or 'know', the other, reflecting that aspect of empathy as 'self-alienation' which troubled Husserl (1970b, p. 189 in Zahavi, 2003, p. 124). The asymmetry between self-experience and other-experience appears to be a 'necessary and persisting existential fact' (Zahavi & Rochat, 2015, p. 544), but one which we seem to repeatedly lose sight of.

Empirical method, phenomenology, and psychotherapeutic research

Empirical findings appear more like signposts that point towards sensual meaning but do not show it. Instead, the sense of phenomenology we have described here shows the sensual more clearly. Being phenomenological in this sense appears to 'open up' language, so that the differences between sensual and given meaning appear. Being phenomenological in this way encourages us to take seriously the questioning of experience, rather than fall too easily into the captivity of 'given' ideas and beliefs, and assumptions.

Giorgi's (2009) method may reflect a way people speak in the 'natural attitude' (Husserl, 1927/1971 (19, II, 8) in McCormick and Elliston (1981), as cited in Welton (1999), pp. 329–330) of a discipline, believing they are being more accurate, more scientific, more informed perhaps. But what happens instead is that the more detailed the description becomes in psychological language (the language of his scientific community), the more it just becomes closed off into that psychological language. This also seemed to appear everywhere in the empirical findings, with reference to the 'technical' ('spoken' or 'given') language of psychiatry and psychology being ubiquitous. But there was something else going on which the empirical findings could not access (similarly by default). For example, while the empirical findings indicated that mental health nurses were therapeutic through being with or spending time with a person, the struggle for each participant to speak about what 'being with' meant appeared to expose a certain failure of 'spoken' speech, or 'given' meaning in language. For example, one participant spoke about what was therapeutic as 'all about that interaction and having that rapport with someone ... and building on that kind of relationship with that person ...'. But she struggled to speak about this much further, as if the words did not come easily, or could not be found in those she had been given or through which she felt she could speak. It seemed that she needed a place to find her own truthfulness in this struggle for words, and also to come to understand more clearly the ambiguity in words like 'rapport', and 'relationship'. In her general synthesis, this struggle is written as '*the therapeutic is hard to express*', and so, this empirical finding seems to stand like a signpost showing that another journey is needed.

The insistence on looking at the signposts rather than the landscape may explain why van Kaam's 'axiom' (Van Kaam, 1966, p. 32) – that 'identically named experiences refer basically to the same reality in various subjects' (Von Eckartsberg, 1998, p. 14) – is so persistent in psychological research.

Concluding remarks

It appears that we belong in an intersubjectivity, or what Husserl saw as 'co-constituting intersubjectivity' (Husserl, 1960, p. 125 in Zahavi, 2003, pp. 116–117). In effect, we depend on each other, but also, we can become trapped in another's idea, and another may trap us in that idea. The importance of the asymmetrical relationship between people becomes clearer if this 'entrapment' is kept in mind. Making this relationship symmetrical would result in us all being copies, eventually, 'of the same story in a newspaper' (Zahavi, 2003, p. 116, alluding to Wittgenstein's (2009, §265) example).

In being caught up in a theory, or idea (the same story in a newspaper), then we think we can describe the world accurately in our words, without realising that the words have already been provided by the theory. It seems that 'knowing' this is different to coming to know it in one's own 'truthfulness'. It seems that the *act* of 'truthfulness' is what is most important, rather than a repeat of words that define the search for that truthfulness. It appears that this is what mental health nurses who are open to others (and themselves) may show, and offer, to others. This kind of openness is like an invitation for the other person to simply speak of their experience and come to know it in a more truthful way.

Giorgi's (2009) method may make us think that we know something about the person's meanings which can be pinned down and repeated. They *can* be pinned down and repeated only in the sense that 'spoken' speech acts like a reservoir of agreed, given, meanings (Merleau- Ponty, 1945/2014, pp. 202/238), just as Husserl (1973) noted that only 'normal' people define what is normal and that then becomes 'sedimented' into a tradition (Zahavi, 2003, p. 134; Husserl, 1973, p. 162). Instead, we see that the phenomenological opens up a space for another in which she may find her own 'truthfulness' in what seems to be an 'endless openness' (Husserl, 1960, p. 107).

What can be seen from the above phenomenological considerations is also how being phenomenological through 'not knowing', through 'opening up' language, through being open to one's own experience of the experience of trying to be open to the other, is a form of psychotherapeutic research. What we mean here is that being phenomenological in the ways we have noticed is a way of understanding (and of understanding that we don't understand), returning us to a 'knowledge' that stretches the boundaries of our routine and empirical ways of comprehending the other. This is hard work. There is no fixed, comforting way, or method, that will ease the burden of this kind of phenomenological 'thinking', of being open to the other. There is the painful realisation that we may be getting it wrong most of the time, but it is in the phenomenological openness to that 'getting it wrong' that something else is given room, rather than a repeat of words already given that close down our own, and the other's, experience.

Disclosure statement

No potential conflict of interest was reported by the author(s).

References

Cutcliffe, J. R. (2000). Fit for purpose? Promoting the human side of mental health nursing? *British Journal of Nursing, 9*(10), 632–637. https://doi.org/10.12968/bjon.2000.9.10.6275

Eriksen, K. Å., Arman, M., Davidson, L., Sundfør, B., & Karlsson, B. (2013). 'We are all fellow human beings': Mental health workers' perspectives of being in relationships with clients in community-based mental health services. *Issues in Mental Health Nursing, 34*(12), 883–891. https://doi.org/10.3109/01612840.2013.814735

Eriksen, K. Å., Dahl, H., Karlsson, B., & Arman, M. (2014). Strengthening practical wisdom: Mental health workers' learning and development. *Nursing Ethics, 21*(6), 707–719. https://doi.org/10.1177/0969733013518446

Freeman, A. (1993). Operative intentionality: Notes on Merleau-Ponty's approach to mental activities that are not the exclusive product of the conscious mind. *Journal of Phenomenological Psychology, 24*(1), 78–89. https://doi.org/10.1163/156916293X00053

Freud, S. (1915/2001). The unconscious 1914-1916. In J. Strachey (Ed.), *The standard edition of the complete psychological works of sigmund freud – on the history of the psycho-analytic movement, papers on metapsychology and other works* (Vol. XIV, pp. 159-215). Vintage, The Hogarth Press and The Institute of Psychoanalysis.

Giorgi, A. (2002). Lessons for the future from the margins of psychology. *Journal of Phenomenological Psychology, 33*(2), 179-201. https://doi.org/10.1163/15691620260622886

Giorgi, A. (2006). Concerning variations in the application of the phenomenological method. *The Humanistic Psychologist, 34*(4), 305-319. https://doi.org/10.1207/s15473333thp3404_2

Giorgi, A. (2009). *The descriptive phenomenological method in psychology: A modified Husserlian approach*. Duquesne University Press.

Gray, R., White, J., Schulz, M., & Abderhalden, C. (2010). Enhancing medication adherence in people with schizophrenia: An international program of research. *International Journal of Mental Health Nursing, 19*(1), 36-44. https://doi.org/10.1111/j.1447-0349.2009.00649.x

Heaton, J. M. (2010). *The talking cure: Wittgenstein's therapeutic method for psychotherapy*. Palgrave Macmillan.

Heidegger, M. (1930). On the essence of truth. In D. F. Krell (Ed.), *Basic Writings* (2nd ed.). Harper-San Francisco.

Heidegger, M. 1962/2008. *Being and time* (J. Macquarrie & E. Robinson, Trans.). Oxford.

Heidegger, M. (1985). *History of the concept of time: Prolegomena* (T. Kisiel, Trans.). Indiana University Press.

Husserl, E. (1927/1971). Phenomenology – britannica article, fourth draft (Richard E. almer, Trans.). *Journal of the British Society for Phenomenology, 2* (2), 77-90.

Husserl, E. (1952/1989). [Husserliana 4]. *Ideas pertaining to a pure phenomenology and to a phenomenological philosophy, book 2, studies in the phenomenology of constitution* (R. Rojcewicz and A, Schuwer, Trans.). Kluwer Academic Publishers

Husserl, E. (1960). [Husserliana 1]. *Cartesian meditations. An introduction to phenomenology* (D. Cairns, Trans.). Martinus Nijhoff.

Husserl, E. (1962/1977). [Husserliana 9]. *Phenomenological psychology: Lectures, summer semester 1925* (J. Scanlon, Trans.). Martinus Nijhoff.

Husserl, E. (1969). *Formal and transcendental logic* (Dorion Cairns, Trans.). Martinus Nijhoff.

Husserl, E. (1970a). [Husserliana 19] *Logical Investigations*. (J. N. Findlay, Trans.). Routledge & Kegan Paul

Husserl, E. (1970b). [Husserliana 6]. *The crisis of european sciences and transcendental phenomenology: An introduction to phenomenological philosophy* (D. Carr, Trans.). Northwestern University Press.

Husserl, E. (1973). [Husserliana 15]. *Zur Phänomenologie der Intersubjektivität. Text aus dem Nachlass. Zweiter Teil: 1929-1935* (I. Kern Ed.). Martinus Nijhoff.

Husserl, E. (1982). [Husserliana 3]. *Ideas I. Ideas pertaining to a pure phenomenology and to a phenomenological philosophy, first book, general introduction to a pure phenomenology* (F. Kersten, Trans.). Martinus Nijhoff.

Jones, M. (2009). The side effects of evidence-based training. *Journal of Psychiatric and Mental Health Nursing, 16*(7), 593-598. https://doi.org/10.1111/j.1365-2850.2009.01401.x

Kristeva, J. (1982). *Powers of horror: An essay on abjection* (L. S. Roudiez, Trans.). Columbia University Press.

McCormick, P., & Elliston, F. (1981). *Husserl: Shorter works*. University of Notre Dame Press.

McSherry, A. (2018). *What is the need, if any, for therapeutic education in mental health nursing? An empirical phenomenological study of mental health nurses' responses to this question* [Unpublished PhD thesis]. Research Centre for Therapeutic Education, Dept. of Psychology, Roehampton University.

McSherry, T., Loewenthal, D., & Cayne, J. (2015). The implications of Kristeva's notion of the abject in understanding the significance of therapeutic knowledge and practice in mental health nursing. *Journal of Psychiatric and Mental Health Nursing, 22*(1), 82–88. https://doi.org/10.1111/jpm.12180

Merleau- Ponty, M. (2014/1945). *Phenomenology of perception* (D. A. Landes, Trans.). Routledge.

Merleau-Ponty, M. (1964). *The primacy of perception*. (J. M. Edie, Ed.). Northwestern University Press.

Merleau-Ponty, M. (1968). *The visible and the invisible*. North Western University Press.

Moran, D. (2000). *Introduction to phenomenology*. Routledge.

Polt, R. F. H. (1999). *Heidegger: An introduction*. UCL Press.

Shaw, D. M. (2014). *The operative world: Meaning and understanding in merleau-ponty* [PhD thesis]. University of York. http://etheses.whiterose.ac.uk/7790/

Van Kaam, A. (1966). *Existential foundations of psychology*. Duquesne University Press.

Von Eckartsberg, E. (1998). Existential-phenomenological research. In R. S. Valle (Ed.), *Phenomenological inquiry in psychology: Existential and transpersonal dimensions* (pp. 21–61)). Plenum Press.

Welton, D. (1999). *The essential Husserl: Basic writings in transcendental phenomenology*. Indiana University Press.

Wittgenstein, L. (1998). *Culture and value* (G. H. von Wright with N. Nyman Eds.; A. Pichler & C. Winch, Trans.; rev ed.). Oxford.

Wittgenstein, L. (2009). *Philosophical Investigations* (G. E. M. Anscombe, J. Schulte, & P. M. S. Hacker Eds.; Schulte, J., & Hacker, P. M. S, Trans.; rev. 4th ed.). Wiley-Blackwell.

Zahavi, D. (2003). *Husserl's Phenomenology*. Stanford University Press.

Zahavi, D., & Rochat, P. (2015). Empathy≠sharing: Perspectives from phenomenology and developmental psychology. *Consciousness and Cognition: An International Journal, 36*, 543–553. https://doi.org/10.1016/j.concog.2015.05.008

Zauszniewski, J. A., Bekhet, A., & Haberlein, S. (2012). A decade of published evidence for psychiatric and mental health nursing interventions. *Online Journal of Issues in Nursing, 17*(3), 8.

Finding my voice: Telling stories with heuristic self-search inquiry

Elizabeth Nicholl, Del Loewenthal and James Davies

ABSTRACT
It has been argued that qualitative research can be valuable in providing a forum for the voices of those who may usually be excluded from academic discourse and that it is therefore well suited to exploring individuals' experiences of illness. This article is informed by the authors' research into how people diagnosed with 'schizophrenia' experience their personal therapy. It focuses upon the usefulness of phenomenological research methods for investigating personal experience whilst at the same time considering how these methods might enable the researcher to hear the experience of others. It is proposed that personal stories can be seen as being closer to literature and so something of their essence can be killed off by having to shape them through systematic approaches to research. Therefore, the aim here is to explore whether it is possible or indeed desirable to take a systematic approach to personal experience when conducting psychotherapeutic research and how this might be beneficial or detrimental to researcher and participants.

Introduction

It has been argued that qualitative research is particularly valuable in providing a forum for the voices of those who may usually be excluded from academic discourse and that it is therefore most suited to exploring individuals' experiences of illness (Knight et al., 2003; McCarthy-Jones et al., 2013). Where 'individuals with mental illness are commonly viewed as "different"' (Knight et al., 2003, p. 216) this difference potentially exacerbates feelings of fear and stigma, and so qualitative research can offer these individuals the opportunity to relate their stories of marginalisation. With regard to psychotherapeutic research in general, Loewenthal and Winter (2006) have pointed out the view held since Plato that 'while scientific and technical thinking is important, it should be secondary to the resources of the human soul' (Loewenthal & Winter, 2006, p. xviii). Yet, McLeod (2001) has argued that research can be valuable for talking therapists in that it generates 'new understandings of the therapeutic process, and [enables] the experience of different participants in therapy, particularly clients, to be heard' (McLeod, 2001, p. viii).

This article is informed by the authors' research into how people diagnosed with 'schizophrenia' experience their personal therapy. The lead author's interest in this area of research arose from her own experiences of revealing a diagnosis of 'schizophrenia' in personal therapy. She received this diagnosis in late adolescence and upon recovery, she found that the best means of living a 'normal' life without the risk of ongoing stigma was to hide this diagnosis. However, twenty years after receiving, and then hiding, the diagnosis she commenced a psychotherapy training and was obliged to enter into personal therapy. Despite initial concerns about revealing a history of 'mental illness' there were both supportive and challenging experiences with three psychotherapists seen consecutively and as a result of this, she was interested in whether others who have received a diagnosis of 'schizophrenia' perceived this label as having affected their therapy. These experiences in personal therapy will be explored in more detail later in this article in an extract from the lead author's heuristic self-search inquiry. The extent to which it is true that others have perceived their therapy as having been affected by their label will be the subject of another paper which will look at the content of the stories related by the participants in the lead author's research.

The main focus of this paper will be upon heuristic self-search inquiry (Sela-Smith, 2002, 2013) and what it may offer phenomenological research, particularly when looking at how to relate one's personal experience alongside the experiences of others. In addition, reference will be made to whether it is possible or indeed desirable to take a systematic approach to personal experience when conducting psychotherapeutic research and how this might be beneficial or detrimental to researcher and participants.

There will be a brief overview of relevant literature on this topic before a consideration of how method and literature can be seen to be in tension with one another. Heuristic research and heuristic self-search inquiry will be discussed in some detail; this will be followed by an extract from the lead author's heuristic self-search inquiry. This is included in order to highlight how such a personal account, that could be seen as being closer to literature than a more 'traditional' form of research, can be at odds with what is understood to be a formal, systematic approach to psychotherapeutic research. This article will then conclude with a consideration of how psychotherapeutic research methods can be both beneficial and detrimental for researcher and participants.

Literature

Firstly, it is important to look at what existing research may say about the experiences in personal therapy of people with a diagnosis of 'schizophrenia'. This is because it has a bearing on the lead author's own story, which is told in the heuristic self-search inquiry that follows, and in which the lead author experienced nurturing, healing relationships as well as an experience that was deeply damaging.

It has been argued that psychiatric labels such as 'schizophrenia' bring with them stigma and a sense of marginalisation from society (Hayes, 2013). These issues may then have an impact on the ability to disclose in personal therapy and upon the client's perception of their therapist's response to that disclosure. An important issue is whether client perceptions are indeed perceived to be valid in psychotherapeutic terms, in part because they may be interpreted as symptomatic of the client's psychopathology (Zilcha-Mano et al., 2014). However, in writing about what clinicians can learn from service user memoirs, Armstrong (2012) writes that despite 'distortions and inaccuracies that might undermine particular works … [these] memoirs can provide insight on aspects of patient experience that may be obscured or remain hidden to busy clinicians' (p. 342). When conducting the literature review, however, it became evident that there has been little formal research conducted into the experiences of people diagnosed with 'schizophrenia' in their personal therapy in contrast to a much larger body of literature regarding how psychotherapists experience this work. There are some first person accounts such as those of Greenblat (2012) and Comans (2011) who both stated that their recovery was aided by therapists who listened to them with care and respect. In contrast, Sen (2017) describes a different experience of therapy. As a child she first saw a psychiatrist whom she describes as cold and uncaring; this encounter had a profound effect upon her and she writes about how she wonders if 'my life might have been different if I had met a warm, kind, supportive professional. Maybe my life would have played out the same, but I know I would have experienced a little less pain' (Sen, 2017, p. 91). In adulthood, Sen saw a number of therapists and what seems to be have been important in establishing a therapeutic relationship was the attitude of the therapist rather than their practicing modality. Warmth, care, authenticity and a desire to listen to her experiences as well as a relationship in which the political and social context of the client's world are acknowledged are what Sen found most beneficial in her experiences of psychotherapy.

In summary, although there is little formal research into this area, what seems to emerge from first person stories about having a diagnosis of 'schizophrenia' and being in therapy is that it can help one rediscover who one is when rebuilding one' life post-diagnosis. Feeling respected rather than dismissed for beliefs and behaviours that may appear 'wrong' or 'abnormal' is vitally important (Comans, 2011; Greenblat, 2012; Sen, 2017; Sparrowhawk, 2009). Furthermore, although a diagnosis may initially provide some reassurance to a person experiencing psychosis, this may then have the effect of imposing a medical meaning upon their experience. This kind of meaning tends to impose a narrative of personal failing, which compounds self-loathing and deepens despair. Nor are all psychotherapeutic approaches necessarily helpful, particularly those with the intention of managing symptoms and which '*explain* with theory before attempting to *understand* what was experienced' (Cotton & Loewenthal, 2015, p. 84). These therapies also tend to dictate what is 'normal' and what is not, and they can thus close down any attempt at personal meaning-making when undergoing unusual experiences. What seems to be most helpful is the formation of a connection with a therapist and then being free to explore the meaning a person makes of their experiences without being told what those experiences mean (Cotton & Loewenthal, 2015).

Methodology

The lead author employed narrative analysis alongside heuristics in her doctoral research, but as already stated, the focus of this paper is upon heuristics and so in this section, there will be descriptions of both Moustakas' heuristic research and of Sela-Smith's heuristic self-search inquiry.

Moustakas' heuristic inquiry

In order to comprehend Sela-Smith's (2002, 2013) adaptation of heuristics as a research method it is first necessary to give an overview of Moustakas (1990) heuristic inquiry. Heuristic inquiry is a 'phenomenological research method that focuses on investigating human experience' (Roland Price & Loewenthal, 2007, p. 68); Moustakas (1994) states clearly that throughout the research process the participants remain as close as possible to the phenomenon they have experienced and that in recounting their stories they deepen their understanding of and insights into that phenomenon. Moustakas (1990) described heuristics as a way of discovering and uncovering new understandings of the research topic, with both the researcher and co-researchers gaining in self-knowledge at the same time. 'The heuristic process is autobiographic' (Moustakas, 1990, p. 15) and so the research question ought to be one of profound personal significance to the researcher who remains highly visible throughout the research process. The data lies within the researcher and through both dialogue with others and oneself a story can be created 'that portrays the qualities, meanings and essences of universally unique experiences' (Moustakas, 1990, p. 13). Self-dialogue is important from the beginning of the entire study because 'one's own self-discoveries, awarenesses, and understandings are the initial steps' (Moustakas, 1990, p. 16). By engaging in self-dialogue, the researcher hopes to make their tacit dimensions known to themselves and others. Tacit knowledge, or those things we can sense about the wholeness of an entity through an understanding of its constituent parts, is what underlies the heuristic processes that Moustakas outlines. Moustakas (1990) argues, after Polanyi, that if we put the tacit realm to one side in research then the possibilities of new understandings of a phenomenon are limited and curtailed:

> "The declared aim of modern science is to establish a strictly detached, objective knowledge.... but suppose that tacit thought forms an indispensable part of all knowledge, then the ideal of eliminating all personal elements would, in effect, aim at the destruction of all knowledge" (Polanyi, 1966, p. 20)

There are six phases that the researcher must follow, the first of these being the identification of the research question. The aim of this initial engagement is to discover 'an intense interest, a passionate concern that calls to the researcher, one that holds important social meanings and personal, compelling implications' (Moustakas, 1990, p. 27). After having identified the research question the researcher becomes involved in a process of self-dialogue and introspection in order to engage with the phenomenon as fully as possible. This requires a period of immersion, with the question being lived in both waking and sleeping states. Subsequently, the researcher retreats from this intense focus upon the question in an attempt to allow for an incubation of the knowledge gained from the immersion period. The hope is then that the researcher will be open to their intuitive and tacit understandings of the question which should lead to moments of illumination and new understandings. During the next phase of the study, the researcher describes and explains the phenomenon, developing understandings of the experience and organising them into themes. The final phase involves drawing the themes from the participant interviews together into a creative synthesis, which is often in the form of a narrative depiction, but can also be expressed as a story, an artwork or a poem. Moustakas (1990) claims that this process requires the researcher to be fully present and honest throughout a time-consuming period of 'sustained immersion and focused concentration on one central question, to risk the opening of wounds and passionate concerns, and to undergo the personal transformation that exists as a possibility in every heuristic journey' (Moustakas, 1990, p. 14).

From Moustakas to Sela-Smith

It has been argued that Sela-Smith saw Moustakas' heuristic method as offering the possibility of opening 'a radical shift from the medical model and [allowing] a view of a person who can engage himself or herself in life and make choices, even in the presence of severe personal problems (or diagnosis)' (Ozertugrul, 2017, p. 1). Taking this as a starting point, Sela-Smith developed Moustakas' method of heuristic inquiry. She formulated what she terms Heuristic Self-Search Inquiry (HSSI) as a response to what she sees as the limitations of Moustakas' method, arguing that the final frontier of human knowledge is the internal world, or interiority, an area which has been resisted as a legitimate source of scientific knowledge. Sela-Smith (2002) argues that there is the danger in much heuristic research that the findings will be derived from participants rather than from within the researcher and that there has been a move to an observation of experience rather than being immersed in a self-search. It is proposed that this is because of an ambivalence that is present in Moustakas' writings on heuristic inquiry where he moves from the experience of his own self-search to the observation of an experience. Therefore, the use of participants means that their experience becomes part of the data and the validity of the researcher's experience is therefore 'established by the similar experiences of others'

(Sela-Smith, 2002, p. 76). Sela-Smith (2002) argues against this, suggesting instead that 'coparticipants, if they are used in self-search, are valuable as reflectors of possible areas of resistance that may be out of conscious awareness' (Sela-Smith, 2002, p. 78). This resistance 'is addressed by Sela-Smith as difficulty staying with the *"I-who-feels"* and this acknowledgement is what separates heuristic self-search inquiry from Moustakas' heuristic inquiry' (Tweedie, 2015, p. 49). Checking one's own experience against that of others does not make that experience more valid but using the experience of others to illuminate one's own blind spots has some value. The idea is that others will then experience the researcher's deepening self-awareness through the story the researcher tells. When telling this story it is important for the researcher to speak from the 'I' and to remain connected to the feelings, both past and present, that the experience evokes rather than simply adopting a reporting style.

In Sela-Smith's heuristic self-search inquiry there is, therefore, an emphasis on the feelings of the researcher with the claim that 'within the interiority, feeling responses to external circumstances combine to create meaning, and out of meaning personalities are organized, personal and cultural myths are formed, world views are constructed, and paradigms are set in place' (Sela-Smith, 2002, p. 54). She proposes that whilst language can facilitate interpersonal communications as well as enhance self-awareness, it can also cause a split in the experience of the self. Experiences that cannot be verbalised are driven underground and are then 'disconnected from the verbal-thinking self' (Sela-Smith, 2002, p. 62). She argues that as a result of accessing these felt experiences through a heuristic process they can be reconstructed anew and a transformation in the meaning one makes of one's life can come about. However, if the research topic is one that is personally painful then the researcher may try to resist the heuristic process in an attempt to avoid re-experiencing pain.

Sela-Smith (2013) claims that the central premise of HSSI is that one facilitates self-transformation through self-understanding. This is achieved through the self-searcher examining their feelings and the meanings attached to these feelings. A self-search inquiry may begin when the self-searcher comes to realise that they have a sense of internal uneasiness or disharmony and it 'can begin with an event that impacts a person in a way that causes painful emotion, such as fear, shame, guilt, sadness or grief' (Sela-Smith, 2013, p. np).

In common with all heuristic methods, the six key stages in HSSI are summarised as: the researcher has experience of what is being researched; the researcher has an intense interest in the topic of research and looks inward for tacit knowledge; the researcher lives, wakes, sleeps and dreams the question; the researcher dialogues with the feeling rather than simply reporting it; the research is conducted into oneself; and a story is told of some form of transformation that has taken place, with this story containing the possibility of transforming those who read it (Sela-Smith, 2002). However, she does claim that although HSSI is, in common with any heuristic research, an intuitive process, there is no specific method that one follows in order to conduct it (Sela-Smith, 2013). She states that 'only after enough light is brought in by way of the heuristic process, can theories be postulated, and results predicted and tested using the more traditional "scientific method"' (Sela-Smith, 2013, p. np). Therefore, her view is that as a researcher one must pay attention to one's own experiences and feelings in order to bring about a transformation that can then transform those that read it.

The hope was for this study that a heuristic self-search inquiry would allow the researcher to speak of the difficulty of having been given a diagnosis and of then having hidden it and passed for 'normal' for over twenty years. The desire was to be able to acknowledge this phenomenon throughout her entire being rather than just making an intellectual acknowledgement that assists her in maintaining a distance from the felt experience. As Sela-Smith (2002) has pointed out, a resistance to the heuristic process may indicate a desire to avoid re-experiencing pain.

A heuristic self-search inquiry

Method

According to heuristic research when telling one's story it is important for the researcher to remain connected to the feelings, both past and present, that the experience evokes rather than simply adopting a reporting style, and thus attempting to fully engage with the feelings that this story evokes. It is therefore important at this stage to write from the I. Sela-Smith (2002, 2013) advocates the use of the six processes of heuristic research in HSSI and so this story was written with Moustakas (1990) heuristic processes in mind. The *initial engagement* with the question originates at the very beginning of this research with the desire to respond to the call to investigate my life experiences. I battled to define the question, and to allow it to find me, and this battle continued through and beyond the point where I decided (or was persuaded) that my story could be told alongside those of my participants. I then *immersed* myself in the question, reading articles, watching films and television programmes and making notes about my own experiences throughout this period. This was followed by some time spent reflecting on what I had taken in; this corresponds to what Moustakas (1990) describes as *incubation*. This is where I faltered, doubting that what I had produced so far had any value. However, it was shortly after this that I began to interview my participants and for me this was a really valuable stage. At this point, my personal reflections and preoccupations started to coalesce into a clearer story that was separate from but informed by the stories of others. This was a period of both *illumination* and *explication* where I began to become aware of what was emerging into consciousness as well as beginning to tell the stories that the participants had told me. The *creative synthesis* then followed, which in this article is an abridged exploration of my experience of the research process, of my experiences of undergoing psychosis and diagnosis, and of my work as a psychotherapist. In it I provide my own narrative as well as describing some personal epiphanies, or movements towards uncovering tacit knowledge, that have arisen as a result of conducting this research with others as well as having spent some time in the indwelling and personal reflection that is a requirement of a self-search inquiry such as this. It consists of three parts, 'The researcher as a person', The researcher as 'schizophrenic' and 'The researcher as psychotherapist', and is presented in the first person because it is my story told with my voice.

The researcher as a person

My resistance to this topic was evident from the beginning of the project. For over twenty years I had hidden from the majority of people in my life the diagnosis of 'schizophrenia' that I had received in my late teens. Towards the end of my Masters in Psychotherapy and Counselling, I attended a presentation by a doctoral student who was researching how people diagnosed with 'schizophrenia' made meaning through their recovery. There was something in the first person accounts he presented that moved me to disclose my own experience of 'schizophrenia' in front of some fellow students and, more significantly, some of my lecturers. It was a risk because I dislike inviting the disapproval or pity of others and I had always felt that any disclosure would result in my being seen as a lesser person by others.

When the time came to choose my own doctoral research question I knew that I wanted to look at how therapists experience working with people diagnosed with 'schizophrenia'. At the time I was aware that my own experience of diagnosis was playing a part in this choice of question but given that I preferred to identify as a psychotherapist rather than as a person who had had a diagnosis of 'schizophrenia' I would of course be choosing to look at the experiences of therapists. My experience as a psychotherapist would inform my approach to research and I was interested in hearing how other psychotherapists worked with people who experienced psychosis. I prepared my research proposal and presented to some fellow students the main themes of an initial literature review one week before I was due to submit the proposal to the university research board. It was dull and dry and I bored myself, let alone my audience, with it. I was then asked to describe my own experience and that was when it came to life. I changed my question and then spent two years immersed in reading, dwelling, being the research question.

Throughout this time I was identifying my research question, writing my research proposal, refusing to engage with my own experience of psychosis, rewriting my research proposal, continuing to refuse to engage with my own experience of psychosis, and immersing myself in literature on 'schizophrenia'. However, although I came to be able to tell a good story about my psychosis, the edited highlights, I was still resisting it. It was far easier to pay lip service to it and then to immerse myself back in the academic endeavour of telling a story about how those poor 'schizophrenic' people are so badly treated.

Once I started interviewing participants it became clear that for the majority of them the issue of disclosure in therapy appeared to be an issue sometimes but generally not as important as it had been for me. I began to realise that it was my own sense of shame that was driving this research and that I had assumed that because I had had a bad experience in therapy this was likely to be a universal experience. If I unknowingly had not wanted to face my shame then perhaps I had assumed the participants had been similarly resistant and so had seen their problem as their therapist's lack of acceptance of the label. However, sometimes they may simply have projected their concerns or resistances onto their therapist.

I was really grappling with how I might present the participants' voices in a way that would not result in them being dismissed as mad but I was still resisting my own voice. It was as I commenced the first draft of my discussion chapter that I started to feel quite desperate. There was something missing and I became more and more frustrated with what I was writing; it was dull and it felt as though something needed to break through. I spent some time sitting with these feelings and I became increasingly aware that having heard the stories of other people what I wanted to do now was to tell my story. It had taken nearly five years of waking, sleeping, dreaming and resisting the research question until I was able to acknowledge that this is my story too. I was ready to give myself a voice.

The researcher as 'schizophrenic'
I was bullied throughout my childhood. I ended up with a good group of friends in upper school but that didn't protect me from being bullied. I was mainly picked on for being 'square', because I wore extremely unstylish clothes, and for being 'brainy'. I was generally a very good girl because I had learnt that behaving and obeying made for an easier life.

My interior life was wild, however. I lived in a fantasy world that was richer and more fulfilling than my day to day existence but it overlaid my daily life in a way that made everything more bearable. I could walk home from school and I would see the real world but I could also see the world my mind was conjuring. When I was fourteen, I changed. I had always loved music but this now became a passion. I discovered ska, two-tone, punk and indie music and really wanted to wear the fashions that were allied with the music. That wasn't going to happen. I was still the rather dull good girl who worked hard and dressed sensibly but inside I was a promiscuous, cigarette smoking, drug-taking rebel. I could only be me in a clandestine way and so was really confused and felt very disjointed.

When I was sixteen, after my O-Levels, something shifted and lightened in me but a couple of years later, shortly before my eighteenth birthday, I started feeling very strange indeed. It was a snowy day and my younger brother had gone out to play with friends. I was waiting for my friends to call me to let me know where we were meeting but they didn't and when my brother returned he told me that they had all been out at the usual sledging hill. I imploded.

From then on I experienced a growing distancing between myself and the world, yet at the same time I felt that I was becoming increasingly invaded. My skull felt thin and permeable. It couldn't stop an osmotic flow of my thoughts into other's heads and their thoughts into mine. I had vivid dreams every night, often about death, and became very confused as to whether my day life or my night life constituted reality, or what others took to be reality anyway. The boundaries between dreams and waking life dissolved. People laughed at me and talked about me when I left the house. Above all, I wanted to die. I could no longer tolerate the presence of myself within the flesh that held me. I could not even touch my own body because it disgusted me and I hated it because it was me.

I tried to kill myself.

I came to in a local general hospital and was transferred to a psychiatric hospital on the other side of the county where I was an in-patient for six weeks. I was diagnosed with 'schizophrenia' and prescribed two different antipsychotic drugs.

I liked my label because it gave a name to what I had been experiencing as well as giving me an identity as 'mad' that I was happy to adopt. However, I came to feel that anything I did was interpreted through the lens of the illness and that I had become depersonalised. This feeling increased once I had had a course of ECT; the professionals in charge of my care stated that I was getting better but I just felt different. I was still as blank as I had previously been but at least there was an absence of acute pain.

The following year was one of the most difficult of my life and I only have patchy memories of it. I couldn't read, watch films or connect with other people. Whoever I had been, whatever passions I had had, were somewhere inaccessible within me.

I had been told that I was now a psychiatric patient for life and that would mean having to take medication until I died. Without the knowledge or consent of my psychiatrist, and with the help of my parents, I slowly started to reduce the tablets and after eight months had stopped taking them altogether. However, that left me with the problem of being unable to stop my fortnightly depot injections without medical consent to do so. My parents persuaded my GP to take over my care, mainly by asking him what he would do if it was his own daughter who was going through this, and so over the following six months he reduced and then stopped the depot injections. As the medications left my body I slowly re-emerged into life and in my final appointment with my psychiatrist I revealed what we had done. He was furious and discharged me from his care, saying 'You'll be back!'

I was never back and I learned to lie. I lied to friends, to employers, to midwives, and I lived a 'normal' life for nearly twenty years.

The researcher as a psychotherapist

I lied for nearly twenty years, during which time I worked and had four children. My plan was to train as a nurse once my youngest child started school and so I started working as a healthcare assistant. One of my colleagues suggested that I apply to work at a nearby psychiatric hospital and so I then started work as a mental health support worker. It was my first contact with psychiatric services in nearly twenty years and I really struggled in the first few weeks of working there because I felt I was looking at the future that could have been mine had I not withdrawn from the drugs and escaped the system. I had vivid and disturbing dreams for some time after starting work there. Nevertheless, I started training as a psychiatric nurse but after a year I changed course and began a psychotherapeutic counselling training.

A course requirement was that I had to have personal therapy. This scared me because I was reluctant to reveal my diagnosis to someone I believed would probably judge me as inappropriate to train as a counsellor. However, I found a psychoanalytic therapist I thought I might be able to trust and having told her my story in our first session together my instinct was proved correct. I quickly began to trust her and the relationship I developed with her was both nurturing and healing. I slowly started to work through the shame I felt as a result of my experience of psychosis in my teens. Unfortunately, twenty months into the therapy she became ill very suddenly and had to stop working with immediate effect. She died a couple of years later and I still feel sorrow that she will never know who I am now.

I missed her desperately but needed to find another therapist quickly in order to complete the required number of hours for my training course. I went for an assessment with someone and because I had developed such a good relationship with my first therapist I thought nothing of revealing to her the diagnosis of 'schizophrenia' that I had received at eighteen. My perception was that she seemed alarmed and uncomfortable when I disclosed this but the assessment continued. As we ended, she simply asked me what medication I was taking for my psychiatric illness. I reiterated that the diagnosis had been made many years ago that I had not taken medication since the age of nineteen and that I had spent over twenty years passing as 'normal'. She then informed me that she would have a think about whether she would want to work with me or not and that she would let me know within a couple of days. I left the session with her thinking that she had simply not heard me. She subsequently phoned me to tell me that she didn't think she could work with me. It was not necessarily because of the diagnosis I had received but my feeling was that it was. I found it very traumatic. Not only was I mourning the abrupt end of a caring and containing therapeutic relationship but now I was facing rejection when I had revealed something of myself about which I was only just learning to feel less shame. I felt violated.

I had hidden my diagnosis for so many years and then only revealed it without significant repercussions to those who needed to know – the NHS Trust I worked for and my first therapist – and so I had not anticipated a wholly negative response when disclosing it during an assessment with a new therapist. Having felt judged and unheard by her resulted in my feeling the shame of 'madness' crashing back onto me. This shame was almost subsumed by the pain of having just lost a therapist to whom I was very attached, but as the years passed the pain diminished but the memory of the shame stayed with me and was expressed through this heuristic self-search inquiry.

All this cannot have failed to have had an impact upon my work as a psychotherapist, not least because I can use it as a way of defining myself as a person who claims her own madness whilst not really doing so. I have always liked to think that as a psychotherapist I am not scared of working with people with diagnoses such as 'schizophrenia' and in fact embrace this work. But of course I have been affected by my clients' diagnoses. In embracing this work I too am paying attention to the label and could adopt the role of rescuer. The challenge for me is to not try to rescue my clients from psychiatric services but to listen to their experiences and sit with them in these experiences.

Discussion and conclusion

Sela-Smith (2002) claims that a heuristic self-search inquiry should be conducted with the aim of telling a story about one's personal transformation with the desire to transform those who hear or read it. The lead author told her story of being a researcher, a psychotherapist and a person diagnosed with 'schizophrenia' and examined some aspects of these facets of her experiencing that had hitherto been unacknowledged by herself. Sela-Smith (2002) also argues that the point of conducting research interviews is not in order to check one's own experience against that of others but to illuminate one's own blind spots. It becomes an exercise in learning what one is avoiding about oneself rather than hearing about the phenomenon itself. To an extent, this was a successful endeavour because the author came to realise that where she had assumed that her desire to explore this topic was motivated by a sense of shame and outrage at having been treated with a lack of care when revealing her historic diagnosis during an assessment session with a psychotherapist, it was probably more about having wanted to be heard and not to be seen as simply a label that she had successfully hidden for many years.

However, although it has been suggested that qualitative research can offer people who have been given a psychiatric diagnosis (Knight et al., 2003) the opportunity to relate their stories of marginalization the question arises as to whether any research method really is useful in doing so. For example, as Sela-Smith (2002) claims, a resistance to the heuristic process can be an indication that the individual wishes to avoid re-experiencing emotional pain and so it is possibly for this reason that the researcher chose to interview other people about their experiences, using narrative analysis to analyse these interviews (the findings from these interviews will be discussed in a forthcoming article). This process brought about a profound desire in the lead author to tell her own story, hence the resulting heuristic self-search inquiry. This became a paradoxical and circular process in which her own story both informed and was informed by the stories of her co-participants. The point here is that although heuristic self-search inquiry is a useful method in its own right, in combining it with narrative analysis the lead author hoped to be able to hold that tension between being prompted to examine her own story as a result of hearing those of others, and of being able to give a voice to her co-participants. In addition, where the lead author wanted to tell her own story it had to be done systematically through the lens of another research method rather than as a piece of literature, possibly as a means of legitimising it as a piece of doctoral research.

What, therefore of the resources of the human soul when it appears that technical thinking has primacy? Indeed, as Loewenthal (2019) has stated, the psychological therapies "have a tradition of exploring our work's physis for something that comes out of itself and therefore should not be determined by externally imposed research methods" (Loewenthal, 2019, p. 1).

Nevertheless, despite these possible detrimental effects on the lead author's story, it is also worth considering the benefits heuristic self-search inquiry had for the research project. Firstly, the lead author feels that she benefitted personally from undertaking this form of inquiry. The process she undertook felt like a continuation of work that had been done over several years of personal therapy and of participating in another research project. Secondly, doing a heuristic self-search inquiry provided a means of working through her feelings in order to be able to bracket them. Bracketing, or epoche, refers to the setting aside of one's prejudices, assumptions and experiences as much as possible in an attempt to hear the client (or participant) without bias (Spinelli, 2005). In bracketing her feelings and being clearer about her own story the lead author was enabled to hear her participants' stories whilst being aware of her own blind spots that could otherwise have led her to universalise her personal experience when conducting a narrative analysis of those stories.

Therefore, as was stated in the introduction, it has been argued that scientific thinking ought to be secondary to the human soul (Loewenthal & Winter, 2006) whilst at the same time research is seen as valuable in enabling the experiences of clients and therapists to be told and heard (McLeod, 2001). Neither of these approaches need be mutually exclusive and indeed the research process was illuminating in allowing the lead author to examine some very painful aspects of her experiencing that she had hitherto avoided, as Sela-Smith (2002) might claim this was helpful in illuminating her blind spots. However, it must also be borne in mind that what was produced by the lead author is simply a form of allegiance bias (see, for example, Luborsky, 1975), where she found results that were distorted by her own attachment to a critical existential-analytic approach to psychotherapy.

Nevertheless, it is worth considering that maybe it is just possible to be able to tell one's own and others' stories without killing off something of their essence by having to shape them through systematic approaches to research.

Disclosure statement

No potential conflict of interest was reported by the author(s).

References

Armstrong, N. (2012). What can we learn from service user memoirs? Information and service user experience. *The Psychiatrist*, 36(9), 341–344. https://doi.org/10.1192/pb.bp.111.037523

Comans, K. (2011). Beyond psychiatry: Understanding my own human experience. *Psychosis, 3*(3), 242–247. https://doi.org/10.1080/17522439.2011.602101

Cotton, T. (2015). *'Schizophrenia' and the crisis of meaning: A heuristic exploration of psychotherapeutic experiences of those who have a 'schizophrenia' diagnosis.* Research Centre for Therapeutic Education, University of Roehampton.

Cotton, T., & Loewenthal, D. (2015). Personal versus medical meaning in breakdown, treatment and recovery from 'Schizophrenia'. In D. Loewenthal (Ed.), *Critical psychotherapy, psychoanalysis and counselling: Implications for practice* (pp. pp.77–92). Palgrave MacMillan.

Greenblat, L. (2012). Understanding health as a continuum. In C. W. LeCroy & J. Holschuh (Eds.), *First person accounts of mental illness and recovery* (pp. pp. 14–19). John Wiley and Sons.

Greenwood, D., & Loewenthal, D. (2007). A case of case study method: The possibility of psychotherapy with a person diagnosed with dementia. In D. Loewenthal (Ed.), *Case studies in relational research* (pp. pp. 88–113). Palgrave Macmillan.

Hayes, S. C. (2013). Foreword: Acceptance, mindfulness and psychotic disorders: Creating a new place to begin. In E. M. J. Morris, L. C. Johns, & J. E. Oliver (Eds.), *Acceptance and commitment therapy and mindfulness for psychosis* (pp. xx–xxii). Wiley Blackwell.

Kenny, G. (2012). An introduction to Moustakas's heuristic method. *Nurse Researcher, 19*(3), 6–11. https://doi.org/10.7748/nr2012.04.19.3.6.c9052

Knight, M. T. D., Wykes, T., & Hayward, P. (2003). People don't understand: An investigation of stigma in schizophrenia using interpretative phenomenological analysis (IPA). *Journal of Mental Health, 12*(3), 209–222. https://doi.org/10.1080/0963823031000118203

Loewenthal, D. (2019). Introduction. In D. Loewenthal & E. Avdi (Eds.), *Developments in qualitative psychotherapy research* (pp. pp. 1–11). Routledge.

Loewenthal, D., & Winter, D. (2006). *What is Psychotherapeutic Research?* Routledge.

Luborsky, L. (1975). Comparative studies of psychotherapies. Is it true that "everyone has won and all must have prizes"? *Archives of General Psychiatry, 32*(8), 995–1008. https://doi.org/10.1001/archpsyc.1975.01760260059004

McCarthy-Jones, S., Marriott, M., Knowles, R., Rowse, G., & Thompson, A. R. (2013). What is psychosis? A meta-synthesis of inductive qualitative studies exploring the experience of psychosis. *Psychosis, 5*(1), 5–16. https://doi.org/10.1080/17522439.2011.647051

McLeod, J. (2001). *Qualitative Research in Counselling and Psychotherapy*. Sage.

Moustakas, C. (1990). *Heuristic Research: Design, Methodology and Application*. Sage.

Moustakas, C. (1994). *Phenomenological research methods*. Sage.

Ozertugrul, E. (2017). A comparative analysis: Heuristic self-search inquiry as self-knowledge and knowledge of society. *Journal of Humanistic Psychology, 57*(3), 237–251. https://doi.org/10.1177/0022167815594966

Pletsch, C. E. (1982). Freud's case studies and the locus of psychoanalytic knowledge. *Acta Hispanica Ad Medicinae Scientiarumque Histmiam Illustrandam, 2*, 263–297.

Polanyi, M. (1966). *The tacit dimension*. Doubleday and Company Inc.

Roland Price, A., & Loewenthal, D. (2007). A case of heuristic research: Is counselling/psychotherapy helpful to midwives on breaking bad news to pregnant women? In D. Loewenthal (Ed.), *Case studies in relational research: Qualitative research methods in counselling and psychotherapy* (pp. 67–87). Palgrave Macmillan.

Sela-Smith (2013) *Heuristic self search inquiry – January 2003 – Updated September 2013*. Retrieved May 14, 2019, from http://www.infiniteconnections.us/heuristic-self-search-inquiry-january-2003

Sela-Smith, S. (2002). Heuristic research: A review and critique of Moustakas's method. *Journal of Humanistic Psychology, 42*(3), 53–88. https://doi.org/10.1177/0022167802423004

Sen, D. (2017). What stays unsaid in therapeutic relationships. *Psychosis, 9*(1), 90–94. https://doi.org/10.1080/17522439.2016.1270988

Sparrowhawk, I. (2009). Recovering from psychosis: Personal learning, strategies and experiences. *Psychosis, 1*(1), 73–81. https://doi.org/10.1080/17522430802588410

Spinelli, E. (2005). *The interpreted world: An introduction to phenomenological psychology* (2nd ed.). Sage.

Tweedie, K. L. (2015) *Relinquishing knowing and reclaiming being: A heuristic self-search inquiry of becoming a counsellor through learning to tolerate uncertainty by reflecting on experience in life, counselling practice and research* [Unpublished Doctoral Thesis]. University of Edinburgh.

Zilcha-Mano, S., Mccarthy, K. S., Dinger, U., & Barber, J. P. (2014). To what extent is alliance affected by transference? An empirical exploration. *Psychotherapy, 51*(3), 424–438. https://doi.org/10.1037/a0036566

'When working in a youth service, how do therapists experience humour with their clients?'

Patricia Talens

ABSTRACT

'Humor can be dissected as a frog can, but the thing dies in the process and the innards are discouraging to any but the pure scientific mind.' E.B. White (1999., p. 303). How we understand humour in psychotherapy is a challenge to explore, due to the ways in which we obtain knowledge, and risk a dissection that could cause the death of the phenomena itself. The following work attempts to explore the phenomena through detailing from experience. The study explores therapists lived experience of humour when working with young clients.

The researcher collected data from seven therapists, from which the essential essence of the experience was drawn out using a discovery orientated approach. The therapists experienced humour as emotional, temporal and multi-faceted, with an ability to convey multiple meaning simultaneously.

Humour was seen to facilitate relational desires which may not feel acceptable or appropriate to vocalise within the therapeutic relationship. Through humour, friendship, anger, maternal care, sexual desire and role modelling, all found expression which gave therapists material to reflect upon. Thus, the present study suggests that humour can function as a haven for feelings that neither the therapist nor young person feel able to address.

Introduction

Humour is considered ubiquitous and universal, entering most aspects of modern-day culture. Its many strands of theory and numerous attempts for definition, demonstrate its allusive and flexible nature. More recently, therapy is attempting to *use* what it knows about humour and how it knows this to maximize its use in analysis (Allen & Reynes, 1987; Franzini, 2001; Middleton, 2007; Richman, 1996; Sultanoff, 2013). However, there is a concern amongst some therapists towards misguided uses, due to a lack of awareness regarding what humour communicates in that moment.

Within the literature lies a vast quantity of clinical cases (Brigitte et al., 2013; McGhee, 1971a) offering examples of how humour is used, but which can be problematic as they predominantly come from observational perspectives. This often leaves out or fails to account for the observer's relationship with humour, forgoing understanding of how their interpretation affects what is seen or felt. Instead, observations are focussed on identifying concepts already established within existing theories. Whilst this may be valuable for validity and evidence, discourse rarely moves far from established thought.

Key to the research is a relational approach that gives voice to the lived experience within the relationship, rather than a pre-determined study based on individual psyche. The study goes on to give priority to the therapist's experience of humour when working with young clients, using a discovery-orientated approach. Its primary focus is the experience of seven therapists who all work within a youth setting that provide counselling services to young people aged 11–25.

By the word 'therapist', the study is speaking in specific relation to talking therapies. It considers all therapists who are working as counsellors, psychotherapists and any other counselling modality that is recognised by UK governing bodies within talking therapy. Literature that specialises in speech therapy or physical therapy with youth will be excluded. The term 'humour' in this study will use the Oxford Dictionary Online (2016) definition: 'the quality of being amusing or comic, especially as expressed in literature or speech' or 'a mood or state of mind' as stated in the introduction. The literature for the review was sourced from EBSCOhost and Google Scholar search engines, in which keywords were run in combination. Keywords were: 'humour', 'psychotherapy', 'counselling', 'youth', 'adolescent', and 'play'.

Literature Review

When considering humour in psychotherapy, there is a large body of work within the psychoanalytical field, which has its foundations in the work of Sigmund Freud. For Freud (2002), jokes like dreams, would require interpretation as they both came disguised from the 'unconscious'. His work began by highlighting a gap in literature, that focused heavily on 'superiority theory', rooted in the works of Plato and Aristotle (Morreall et al., 2014). As the 'superiority theory' suggests, its core concept is that the amusing object is considered inferior whilst the subject casting the ridicule is given a position of superiority in direct relation to it.

With the age of modernity and a propensity towards science, ideas about humour turned to theories geared towards the individual and away from the relational. With extensive theorising by Freud, much of the initial literature is dominated by psychoanalytic perspectives which still hold weight in current studies. His work on jokes is considered an expansion of his theories relating to dreams and concepts of the 'unconscious' as he highlights how their similarities 'all show a far-reaching agreement with the processes of the "dream-work".' (Freud, 2002, p. 156). If both dreams and jokes came from the 'unconscious', then they could serve as a gateway into uncovering material of the individual. Therefore, humour is thought of as a way of accessing regressed painful feelings, and so jokes could be analysed in the same manner as dreams and developed into a technique for analysis.

Vaillant (1977) would go on to categorise humour as a mature defence, highlighting its ability to cope with stressors in a sophisticated manner that allows for the highest level of gratification. Lothane (2008) adds that humour is considered well suited in 'loosening repression, facilitating the emergence of unconscious emotions and ideas' (p. 232). From this, the analyst goes on to provide sympathy and acceptance, which in turn allows the client 'to overcome his denial and rise to a higher level of insight and personal growth' (p. 234). Linking this idea of growth to the individual's creativity, Marcus states that 'integrating spontaneous ideation which originally seems absurd, is what links humour and creativity' (Marcus, 1990, p. 431). Furthermore, developments took place regarding the idea of humour as being multi-layered in meaning. The concept that one message is consciously conveyed whilst the other reveals unknown and unconscious feelings. It is thought to have the 'ability to produce verbal communication *and* contradictory non-verbal signals simultaneously' (Panichelli, 2013, p. 438). From this, humour is thought of as a social lubricant, facilitating conversations which may ordinarily feel too risky to communicate. The basis of this idea gives emphasis on how the therapeutic relationship benefits from such communications. It is considered to be a strong mechanism for developing, understanding and conveying empathy even when culture and upbringing shapes our sense of humour differently (Middleton, 2007). This aspect makes it possible to consider humour as universal and available to the therapist in all situations. Often, described as a tool towards the therapeutic process, and for a potential assessment tool in the future (Allen & Reynes, 1987).

Emerging, is a consistent theme and move towards humour being viewed as a tool or technique. With definitions of therapeutic humour as the 'intentional and spontaneous use of humour techniques by therapist and other health professionals, which can lead to improvements in the self-understanding and behaviour of clients or patients' (Franzini, 2001, p. 171). This is thought possible because humour facilitates difficult and challenging feelings by reducing the level of anxiety (Franzini, 2001; Sultanoff, 2013). However, Richman (2006–2007) argues for the need to have a well-established relationship in the therapy room for humour to achieve its full potential, and that the working alliance is a 'collaboration that involves the participation of both parties' (p. 43). Richman (1996) offers other advantages in the form of safe risk taking through play and highlights its' important role if a person wishes to explore, 'In therapy, a humorous attitude is a form of mental play with a serious purpose, to combine self-understanding with the emergence of forbidden or unacknowledged thoughts in a socially acceptable manner' (p. 561). An illustration of this would be to consider the six necessary and sufficient conditions developed by Rogers (1957), which are needed to produce therapeutic change in the client. Sultanoff (2013) considers these conditions in direct correlation with humour by discussing the skills and behaviours of the therapist as well as the client. He argues that the practitioners must firstly be skilled with humour whilst embodying the central conditions of empathy, congruence and positive regard. Finally concluding that 'therapeutic humour can add to a skilled clinician's repertoire of clinical interventions and, like all other skill interventions used in the helping relationship, offered by the therapist based on his clinical judgment' (p. 397).

Kubie (1971) points to the potential for humour to be a destructive force and the danger of how laughing with a client may reinforce their neurotic defences. But Richman (1996) distinguishes *'wit'* from therapeutic laughter, arguing that the latter is a 'recognition of our common humanity' (p. 565) and furthermore is considered kind and tolerant. Although he is aware of and in agreement with Kubie's apprehensions, of a therapist's self-concern over their patients, he argues that humour is an essential tool to uncover 'the vice and folly of the therapist as well as the patient' (Richman, 1996, p. 566). Arguing that there are similarities in both humorous and non-humorous interventions and that in either case, the therapist requires empathy and intuitive timing as well as an awareness of their use. However, these reflections are often considered in relation to adults whilst literature regarding young people lacks equal thought.

When considering humour with young people, terminology and theories orientate towards the role of play and playfulness. There is a shift from psychological frameworks associated with adults, to frameworks of learning, development and education. Often, play and humour overlap in literature due to theories and concepts tending towards specific groups based upon ages and stages in life. This posed a problem when attempting to look at literature that focused on humour with younger clients, as results would frequently relate to the educational domain for its analysis. In some cases, however, a combination of professions appears to yield literature that can cross over concepts and take a wider perspective. Rutherford (1994) gives perspectives as both a therapist and professor and applies her knowledge of humour within a psychotherapeutic environment, to an educational setting: 'frequently, humour soothes a discussion that otherwise may be too intense to be productive' (p. 207).

Work with children can translate to adult work but rarely do we see the opposite happen. Winnicott (1971) is perhaps a notable example of someone who can consider his work with children and the parallels it offers with adults during therapy. Providing a much-needed bridge over from playfulness of children to playfulness of adults in therapy, 'I suggest that we must expect to find playing just as evident in analyses of adults as it is in the case of our work with children. It manifests itself, for instance, in the choice of words, in the inflections of the voice, and indeed in the sense of humour' (p. 54). Winnicott (1971) advocates this state of play and the role of the therapist to permit this, or even encourage it, 'psychotherapy has to do with two people playing together. The corollary of this is that where playing is not possible then the work done by the therapist is directed towards bringing the patients from a state of not being able to play into a state of being able to play' (p. 51). But how accessible is this state of play when studies are orientated around interventions and their outcomes as validation. This can impact on the qualitative or experiential data available, as often studies are geared towards 'evidencing' their results, rather than what emerges within the relational process Dunnes et al. (2000). There are currently approximately 230 approaches and interventions towards working with young people. Forcing a heavy emphasis on techniques and outcomes rather than consideration for the process (Kazdin, 1995a).

Methodology

The literature has highlighted an emphasis on theoretical and observational knowledge obtained predominantly from clinical case studies. The distinct lack of first-hand experiential data has prompted a qualitative and phenomenological approach to the question, as phenomenology is focussed on elucidating meanings from the lived experience of a situation, Valle (1998). In this case, the lived experience of a therapist working in a youth setting.

Phenomenology offers an alternative understanding which can help deepen our comprehension of a given situation. Take for example, how we comprehend a minute of time. Time can be measured by science and quantified, but the experience of time can be vastly different from one person to the next, i.e. one minute may be experienced as long and slow by one person or quick and fast by the next. The experience, for Husserl (2014), would be telling of a person's 'essential structure of consciousness' and would highlight the meaning with a thorough description of their experience. The argument for Husserl was not that the natural sciences were wrong but that it merely constituted part of our understanding, and with that there needed to be a way of accessing other knowledge from human experience. Highlighting the risks of an unreflective and habitual science which is not able to see its constituted attitudes. This eidetic stance is why description of lived experience is of such high value within phenomenology, as there is an attempt to understand how the phenomena in each situation presents itself through us.

Method and Design

Analysis was conducted on data from seven participants following A. Giorgi's (1997) 'descriptive phenomenological approach' (DPA). A. Giorgi (1997), gives us a five-step approach to conducting the research. Firstly, data collection required a minimum of three participants as addressed by A. Giorgi (2008), to provide enough variation for a typical essence to be established. However, emphasis is placed on the quality of the data as opposed to the number of participants. With time limitations considered, a maximum of eight participants was decided for the investigation to have sufficient breadth and depth. One to one interview's lasted approximately one hour for detailed data and used semi structured open-ended questions.

A reading of all the data took place to develop a sense of the whole before constituting into meaning units. Method of division requires the researcher to read through the data highlighting any moments where they feel a transition in meaning. This is an intuitive process in which it is asked of the researcher that they hold firstly, a phenomenological attitude but also justify and stipulate why they have made a discrimination of meaning.

Once meaning units had been established, the process of 'free imaginative variation' could begin. This stage is indicative of the priori stance taken up by the descriptive phenomenological approach. Free imaginative variation puts the meaning units through a process of questioning in order to identify what is necessary to that phenomena. This deductive process aims to establish the essential essences and structure of consciousness for the given phenomena. The researcher then transforms and prepares the data for the given discipline. A. Giorgi (1997), asks that the researcher attempt to use language which is phenomenally grounded staying faithful to the participants' first-hand account.

The final stage of the process gathers and synthesises the meaning units to present a structure or several structures. A. Giorgi (1997) stipulates the importance of not trying to fit everything into one structure but instead to allow as many structures to emerge as needed. It is important to note that these structures are what presented themselves within the research and are not to be considered as conclusive findings: 'the result is not a definition of the phenomenon, but a careful description of the structure of the lived experience of that phenomenon in a particular type of situation' (A. Giorgi, 1997, p. 41).

Findings

Participant 1

Essence: humour is an emotion

Humour presents itself as a form of emotion which is felt as a lightness, and which offers relief from emotionally difficult moments, or moments of stuckness. The emotion can create a shift from intense and difficult feelings. It is experienced as a form of emotional flexibility, which indicates to the therapist, something about their client's current emotional state and their ability to move from this state. The therapist relates this both to their client and themselves 'I think that it is an important part of how I look after myself, that I have a space where I feel lighter. It is something that I do as a defence against some of the more painful things that might come up in a session'. For the therapist, this emotion is intimate, revealing and communicating something about a person, as part of a relational process.

Participant 2

Essence: humour holds power
Humour appears as a purpose lead activity in which the client can express and communicate something to the therapist. Through humour the therapist experienced releasing of sexual tension as well as aggressive tension, which can cause arousal and discomfort for the therapist. For the therapist, humour can carry powerful feelings of aggression and sex which may otherwise not be spoken about. It can be used both as an attack and as a way of diffusing difficult and painful feelings 'A little bit of humour can be used to diffuse all that and take away the anger in a sense'. Humour is predominantly lead with purpose by one person and felt by the other. This purpose can at some point be identified but is not always immediately obvious and requires consideration. 'Humour can be used to get people to like you.' shortly followed with 'But there's also, with him maybe something aggressive about it'.

Participant 3

Essence: humour connects
The therapist experiences humour as a form of connection with the other and describes the emotional contact during moments of shared laughter. Within that connection there are feelings of sexual desire which feel too difficult and intense to speak of, due to this the therapist has considered ending the client work previously. Boundaries of the relationship are experienced as 'pushed' and tested using humour. Humour in the session is the result of what arises between the therapist and client in which something is communicated without words. An authenticity of feelings is revealed through the shared laughter and at times is described as spontaneous and difficult to contain the rupture of laughter that wants to escape. At times, the humour feels too much for the therapist to manage and distracts them from their role as a therapist. The therapist experiences humour as a form of nonverbal communication and playfulness, however within that the therapist is very aware of their professional role as one of guiding and teaching the client a more verbal way of expressing their feelings.

Participant 4

Essence: humour is deceiving

Humour is experienced as a way in which hidden meanings and feelings can be masked and not present. They describe humour as having dual meaning in which something is presented that does not accurately represent the true feelings and thoughts of the person expressing the humour. Humour presents as a defence in the sense that it disguises and masks what the therapist describes as true feelings, either to the world or at times to oneself. The therapist is very aware of their role in a professional capacity and considers unmasking the true feelings as part of their work with the client. The defence is described as armour and the therapist speaks of disarming the client in a gentle way.

Participant 5

Essence: humour is adaptive to situations

Humour can adapt and be present in different situations and settings which indicates the ability for several uses. An example is provided below to illustrate this.

The therapist experiences a client's humour as a way of easing painful emotions and defending against damaging exposure in which the client may not be ready to speak of their difficulties. It is described as 'survival humour' in which clients can cope with trauma due to the humour. In relation to young clients, humour is felt as a mask in which they can present something other than what they are feeling. Within the therapist's own personal therapy, humour was experienced as a deep contact and unity, in which the laughter is described as authentic and spontaneous. Sexual feelings are conveyed and experienced by the therapist in their own therapy, but this is not experienced in the client work.

Within the youth setting, the therapist only has experience of shared laughter when something external has happened which has made both the client and therapist laugh together. Humour can change meaning for the therapist depending on the situation and setting. It is felt that it is possible to facilitate difficult messages in a safe manner as it is communicated with a smile and therefore distanced from true meaning, for this reason the therapist experiences caution towards the use of humour in sessions. Again, within their own personal therapy, shared laughter provided intimacy and came from the relationship, not externally.

Participant 6

Essence: humour is relaxing and comforting

Humour presents as a way in which contact is established with the client and can be a way of speeding up the process of therapy. They describe it as a tool in which they can help the client relax more and therefore facilitate the therapeutic process. 'I feel like I just want to make them more comfortable, that it's ok, or like you should be relaxed. In comparison to adults I wouldn't really do that. I want them to feel more relaxed. I feel like young people are a bit harder to open up'. They describe their experience of humour as coping with difficult emotions and situations. Humour is experienced differently depending on age and setting as it holds different meanings for the therapist. Time also appears as a factor in changing the meaning of humour for the therapist, as they experience humour changing with the dynamic of the client-therapist relationship. 'I think that if we had kept on laughing, then we wouldn't have gotten to the real feelings, I think it changed a bit'.

Participant 7

Essence: humour is relational

For the therapist, humour provides an avenue with which both verbal and nonverbal expressions can be communicated. It has an ability to convey several different meanings which can change over time and through the development of the relationship. The therapist experiences humour as a liveliness in which they feel happiness and joy. They relate humour to an expression of friendship and often feel the client attempting to create a friendship with them beyond the boundaries of the therapeutic relationship. 'They are quite lonely, there is that fantasy that you could be like a friend, and something more outside the therapists' room'. Humour within the sessions is informed by training and expectations of their professional role. 'I think it's just that realisation that there is a boundary as well, that as well as you get along with people in therapy, you're not there to be their friend'.

Synthesis of Participants

Essence: humour is communication and physical expression

Having carried out free imaginative variation on all the data, humour presented itself as a physical expression in the form of a smile, smirk, giggle or laughter from either the therapist or the client throughout all the data. Humour also presented as a form of communication, in the sense that it expressed something whether verbal or nonverbal. These were the essences which were found at the final stages of the findings.

Discussion

The communication of multi-layered meanings is heavily represented in the literature from Freud (1927) to Panichelli (2013), who speaks of humour's 'ability to produce verbal communication *and* contradictory nonverbal signals simultaneously' (p. 438). In the present study, humour provided the ability to communicate something which felt difficult to bring into the room and the relationship. Experienced as a way of exploring difficult emotions which may feel too direct, therapists identified clients using humour as a protective layer. This protection could be harnessed to distract, move away from and defuse tensions that the client or therapist may not be ready to consider. Therapists would describe the experience of their client masking true feelings, and incongruity between what was being said and what was being conveyed. This gives an indication that humour may provide safety when communicating something that feels risky, coinciding with literature of humour as a social lubricant and facilitative of conversations (Rutherford, 1994), with potential to communicate something not desirable by the therapist, client or external agency. Often described, is the experience of release from intense moments during session using humour. This offers a sense of feeling lighter, giving space for emotional movement and a reframing. Panichelli (2013), discusses the importance of helping clients reframe their perspective in which they can experience their situation differently. This is significant when considering the literature, as the findings within this study suggest humour as emerging from the relational dynamic as opposed to a fixed understanding of an individual. This is far removed from concepts of humour as a tool or intervention. Theoretical works of Freud tend to focus on humour's use for obtaining insight and unconscious revelations of an individual's psyche. The role of the humourist and the role of the hearer is examined, but what is less considered is what humour tells us about the relationship and how it changes.

To explore this further, the researcher draws special attention to participant 5. During the interview, the clients' use of humour was experienced as a way to mask feelings of hurt and pain, a common theme seen in many of the other interviews. Within this, it appears the therapist appreciates humour's protective value, but would essentially seek to establish a reduction of humour as they felt this to be more in line with their professional role. The term 'professional' is highlighted as a factor in the study, as the findings refer to the therapist's professional role being significant in their agenda. It brought to light that humour provides a way of communicating not only within the relationship but also about the relationship. Therapists became aware of clients attempting to establish a relationship outside of their 'professional' therapeutic boundaries by changing the dynamic. There were feelings of boundaries being pushed as humour was employed in expressing feelings of anger, sexual desire and friendship.

Within the findings it appeared that humour could adapt to any given situation. For example, therapist 5 spoke of their own personal therapy which presented humour in a vastly different light to the humour with their clients. Instead of masking painful feelings in the way they experience with their clients, humour emerged as a sexually charged connection within their own personal therapy. Feelings of intimacy and unity were expressed non-verbally, providing a release of sexual tension. This raises questions regarding difficulties a therapist may experience when there are high levels of emotional contact and intimacy with their younger clients. Other therapists experienced similar outbreaks of laughter when encountering sexual attraction that was unspoken but felt. Sexual experiences of humour within the study appear to be an increasingly difficult meaning to address with clients. It might even prove difficult to write about as the literature available appears also to move away from the topic. Within the literature, humour is considered to allow a release of tension, most notably from anxiety which in turn makes it possible to facilitate difficult and challenging feelings (Franzini, 2001; Sultanoff, 2013). Therapists can experience difficulties in finding a balance of authenticity within their professional roles and at times are unable to name or reflect on what is happening in the room. In one case, therapist 3 contemplated ending the therapeutic work, rather than addressing the attraction expressed within the humour and relationship. What is described here is a sexual tension that has not been verbally acknowledged. Discomfort is experienced and associated with their disapproval from feelings of arousal towards their client.

The idea of safety felt significant and appeared to be core to the therapists' experience, not just in conveying difficult messages but also, safety within the organisational setting itself. What comes from this is an awareness of how settings and environments such as prisons, schools and charities, may all have an influence on feelings of safety in talking to the therapist and vice versa. Therapists experienced difficulties and confusion regarding their role when having more than one setting, for example, a counselling service within a school or a therapist within a prison. Often therapists were reluctant to use humour with their clients due to fears that it would not appear professional. In contrast, when speaking of experiences within youth work, it appeared that a professional stance was perhaps less desired and therefore allowed humour to be more present in the relationship. The expression of humour was felt to change over time and its dynamic character was able to serve several purposes which felt beneficial to therapists who are comfortable with humour. For the researcher, the institutional setting of the therapy appears to be significant and so further research and expansion on this is of interest.

Humour presented throughout all participant data as a physical movement which communicated or expressed some form of meaning. Central to this is humour's ability to be both verbal and nonverbal. Humour has an ability to demonstrate a different meaning to that which is verbally being said, and therefore, considering not *what* is said in the room but *how* it is said. However, it is this dynamic that makes humour open to interpretation, lending itself to the therapist's own history and experience. Understanding one's own relationship to humour can and did throughout the interviews, provide reflection for participants who felt they had lacked giving humour significant consideration in relation to their work.

Finally, in considering the research method, the study questions DPA's suitability as a method to fully explore findings, when emphasis is placed on description as opposed to interpretation. DPA's strong focus on the adoption of a phenomenological attitude opens the study to a world of possibilities which bring about a rich and fruitful array of findings. Whilst discovery-orientated, its systematic approach strips away participant data. For this reason, it does not feel that DPA takes full advantage of its potential for discovering much more than an essence.

DPA feels both informative and accessible with a large body of work dedicated to its development. In giving such prominence to DPA's philosophical underpinnings, A. Giorgi (2008) provides much clarity and a strong foundation, which could be considered useful for a novice researcher finding their bearings in a complex mixture of qualitative methods. However, despite much clarity, the method is left wanting on other aspects, such as understanding what is meant by disciplinary language. A. Giorgi (1997) himself states 'with all of the human sciences, a consensual common language is not yet an achievement. Rather one confronts competing theories and schools of thought' (p. 8). This creates difficulty when considering language as a set of cultural mores. The idea of defence, emotion, deceit and so forth, are all concepts which are bound up in language and therefore become subject to cultural and temporal context. In reducing the data to such a degree, and by not truly describing the full narrative of that data, these concepts become open to interpretation and subject to the research.

Disclosure statement

No potential conflict of interest was reported by the author(s).

References

Allen, A., & Reynes, R. (1987). Humour in psychotherapy: A view. *American Journal of Psychotherapy, XLI*(2), 260–270. https://doi.org/10.1176.appi.psychotherapy. 1987.41.2.260

Brigitte, K.,Hirsch, R., Jonitz, M., Junglas, K. (2013). Evaluation of a standardized humor group in a clinical setting: A feasibility study for older patients with depression. *International Journal of Geriatric Psychiatry, 28*(8), 850–857. https://doi.org/10.1002/gps.3893

Dunnes, A., Thompson, W., & Leitch, R. (2000). Adolescent males' experience of the counselling process. *Journal of Adolescents, 23*(1), 79–93. https://doi.org/10.1006/jado.1999.0300

Franzini, L. R. (2001). Humour in therapy: The case for training therapists in its uses and risks. *The Journal of General Psychology, 128*(2), 170–193. https://doi.org/10.1080/00221300109598906

Freud, S. (1927). Humour. In J. Strachey (Ed.), *The standard edition of the complete psychological works of sigmund freud, volume xxi (1927-1931): The future of an illusion, civilization and its discontents, and other works* (pp. 159–166). London, UK: The Hogarth Press and the institute of Psycho-analysis.

Freud, S. (2002). The Joke and its Relation to the Unconscious. *Translation and editorial by Joyce Crick, with an introduction by John Carey*. London, UK: Penguin Group.

Giorgi, A. (1997). The theory, practice, and evaluation of the phenomenological method as qualitative research. *Journal of Phenomenological Psychology, 28*(2), 1–17. https://doi.org/10.1163/156916297X00103

Giorgi, A. (2008). Concerning a serious misunderstanding of the essence of the phenomenological method in psychology. *Journal of Phenomenological Psychology, 39*(1), 33–58. https://doi.org/10.1163/156916208X311610

Husserl, E. (2014). *Ideas I*, Translated by. (D. Dahlstrom ed). Hackett.

Kazdin, A. (1995). Child, parent and family dysfunction as predictors of outcome in cognitive-behavioral treatment for antisocial children. *Behaviour Research and Therapy, 33*(3), 271–281. https://doi.org/10.1016/0005-7967(94)00053-M

Kubie, L. (1971). The destructive potential of humour in psychotherapy. *The American Journal of Psychiatry, 127*(7), 861–866. https://doi.org/10.1176/ajp.127.7.861

Lothane, Z. (2008). The uses of humour in life, neurosis and in psychotherapy: Part 2. *International Forum of Psychoanalysis, 17*(4), 232–239. https://doi.org/10.1080/08037060701549861

Lynch, G., & Surf, A. (1999). Exploring young people's perceptions relevant to counselling: A qualitative study. *British Journal of Guidance & Counselling, 27*(2), 231–243.

Marcus, N. (1990). Treating those who fail to take themselves seriously: Pathological aspects of humour. *American Journal of Psychotherapy. 44*(3), 423–432. https://doi.org/10.1176/appi.psychotherapy.1990.44.3.423

McGhee, P. (1971a). Cognitive development and children's comprehension of humor. *Child Development, 42*(1), 123–138. https://doi.org/10.2307/1127069

Middleton, W. (2007). Gunfire, humour and psychotherapy. *Australasian Psychiatry*, *15*(2), 148–155. https://doi.org/10.1080/10398560601148358

Morreall, J., Surf, A. L., & Lynch, G. (2014). Humor, philosophy and education. *Educational Philosophy and Theory*, *46*(2), 120–131. https://doi.org/10.1080/00131857.2012.721735

Oxford Dictionary Online (2016). Oxford University Press. Available at: http://www.oxforddictionaries.com/definition/english/humour (Accessed: 15 January 2016).

Panichelli, C. (2013). Humour, joining, and reframing in psychotherapy: Resolving the auto-double-blind. *The American Journal of Family Therapy*, *41*(5), 437–451. https://doi.org/10.1080/01926187.2012.755393

Richman, R. (1996). Points of correspondence between humour and psychotherapy. *Psychotherapy*, *33*(4), 560–566. https://doi.org/10.1037/0033-3204.33.4.560

Richman, R. (2006-2007). The role of psychotherapy and humour for death anxiety, death wishes, and aging'. *OMEGA*, *54*(1), 41–51. https://doi.org/10.2190/D0NX-7V03-W1H0-4614

Rogers, C. (1957). The necessary and sufficient conditions of therapeutic personality change. *Journal of Consulting Psychology*, *21*(2), 95–103. https://doi.org/10.1037/h0045357

Rutherford, K. (1994). Humour in psychotherapy. *Individual Psychology: The Journal of Adlerian Theory, Research and Practice. 50*(2), 207–222. http://utpress.utexas.edu/

Sultanoff, S. M. (2013). Integrating humour into psychotherapy: Research, theory, and the necessary conditions for the presence of therapeutic humour in helping relationships. *The Humanistic Psychologist*, *41*(4), 388–399. https://doi.org/10.1080/08873267.2013.796953

Vaillant, G. E. (1977). *Adaptation to Life*. Harvard University Press.

Valle, R. (1998). *Phenomenological inquiry in psychology, existential and transpersonal dimensions*. Plenum Press.

White, E. B. (1999). *Essays of E. B. white*. Harper Perennial.

Winnicott, D. (1971). *Playing and reality*. Routledge.

What gets in the way of working with clients who have been sexually abused? Heuristic inquiry

Iana Trichkova, Del Loewenthal, Betty Bertrand and Catherine Altson

ABSTRACT

This article presents the findings of a heuristic investigation of factors that may hinder therapeutic work with people who have been sexually abused. The aim of the researchers was to conduct a study by exploring therapists' lived experience of what may get in the way of working with sexual abuse. For the purpose 8 therapists were interviewed and the collected data was analysed using Heuristic Inquiry. The heuristic inquiry was also based on one of the researchers' personal experience. The study demonstrated that most common hindrances to working with sexually abused clients are therapists' lack of awareness, unresolved personal conflicts or unprocessed traumatic experiences, issues around sex and sexuality, gender stereotypes, lack of experience and inadequate training and supervision. These findings are discussed in terms of their implications for therapeutic work with sexually abused clients. Further research areas are suggested.

Introduction

This study is based on the primary researcher's own experience of working with clients who have been sexually abused, therefore the sections of the article describing the author's experience will be written in the first person. While implementing the various stages of the research process, I realised that for me as a psychotherapist, what came in the way of working with sexually abused clients was unprocessed material around my own history of being sexually assaulted. This was not a quick and easy realisation, but a painful journey, which started with my first and only session with Lucy (all names in this article have been changed for confidentiality purposes). Lucy came to counselling after a long 'career' as a service user of different mental health organisations. She often experienced psychotic episodes and had been diagnosed with schizophrenia. Because of the complexity of her case I had (even though I know there is an argument against doing this) discussions with the service manager and read her assessment very carefully to prepare myself for working with her. I knew she wanted to talk about her 'dysfunctional family' and the sexual abuse she was exposed to in her early teenage years. Looking back now I realise how naïve I was to believe that reading her assessment could prepare me to see and hear Lucy talk about her uncles, who as she put it *'did incest'* on her. She gave me a very detailed and graphic description of what had happened to her, but it was not her words that affected me – in fact they were the exact same words she used during her assessment and I suspected they were a result of her numerous interactions with mental health practitioners. It was the way she said them – she spoke slowly and flatly with a faint, distant smile and even though she did not drop her gaze while talking to me, I could not help but think that the light in her eyes had been extinguished years ago. In front of me was an adult woman whom at that moment I saw as a lost little girl who had endured horrible suffering. I wanted to comfort her and rescue her from her pain (pain that was not visible to me but I assumed was hidden beneath her numbness). I felt powerless and lost, but I also felt the sizzling grip of anger crawling all over me – I was furious at her uncles for using her however and whenever it pleased them, at her mother for not being there for her, at the deranged world we live in for allowing such adversities to happen, and at myself for not knowing how to help her. I became overwhelmed by my reactions and by images that I later realised were reminiscent of my own experience of being sexually assaulted. For what seemed like a long time I stood in front of her stiff and rigid, almost afraid to breathe. I do not know whether she noticed but she did not attend the next session and later sent an email to the service stating that she wanted to discontinue counselling. Maybe Lucy was not ready to have counselling, maybe having one session made her aware that it would be a challenging and painful process. I will never know why she stopped therapy after only one session, but I do know that what she brought to this session evoked something so powerfully frightening and painful for me that I completely disengaged from my client and left her alone with the horror of, and/or arising from the story she was telling me.

My experience in that session with Lucy left me wondering what might get in the way of working with clients who have been sexually abused, which is a question this study sought to answer.

Definitions and previous investigations of the topic

For the purpose of this study sexual abuse is defined as undesired sexual activity in which a person (male or female of any age) is coerced or forced to engage against their will and without their consent.

The study began with a systematic review and thematic analysis (as described by Braun and Clarke (2006)) of the existing academic literature on working with people who have been sexually abused. Most of the literature focuses on how to work with sexually abused clients and gives recommendations on what to do rather than suggest what might hinder the work. Some texts describe how working with sexually abused clients impacts therapists but the emphasis is on the therapists' self-care. These aspects of working with sexually abused clients are important but the aim of this research was to look beyond them and to explore therapists' different experiences and to provide a wider perspective of working with sexual abuse.

These are the relevant themes that emerged from the analysis of the existing academic literature:

Personal experiences and self-awareness

Exposure to clients' traumatic experiences may revive memories of therapists' own exposure to trauma or invalidating experiences (Sanderson, 2013). Lack of self-awareness may affect therapists' ability to hear, acknowledge and be present for the client. Therapists' denial of abuse in their own life may result in conveying a message to the client that it is not safe or acceptable to disclose and discuss their painful experiences. (McBride & Markos, 1994; Sanderson, 1995). Therapists' unresolved conflicts and internalised fears may hinder the therapeutic process, as they may inadvertently impose their personal views and issues on the client or end up using the therapeutic relationship as a mechanism to work further on themselves, rather than focus on the primacy of the client's specific needs (Sanderson, 1995).

Therapists' responses to clients' disclosure of sexual abuse experience

Therapists may be overwhelmed and experience various feelings – anger and hatred, repulsion, fear, helplessness, confusion, shock and horror, grief and sadness, anxiety, guilt and shame (West, 1997). West however also sees danger in a therapist who does not feel anything because such numbness may be an indication that the therapist is not able to empathise with the client. Pearlman and Saakvitne (1995) warn that if therapists' feelings lead the therapy, they may not be able to hear the client and there is a risk of re-enacting previous traumatic situations where the client's feelings and experiences were disregarded.

Therapists may respond to shocking material by finding themselves in disbelief of what they hear (Perlman, 1996). Pearlman and Saakvitne (1995) argue that even the subtlest messages that the therapist does not believe or cannot tolerate what they hear may reinforce the client's fears that their truth is shameful, unspeakable and unbearable to others.

Another response to clients' disclosure of sexual abuse may be voyeuristic interest or even sexual arousal (Pearlman & Saakvitne, 1995). It may evoke anxiety, guilt and shame for the therapist, which may be projected onto the client, who may be seen as seductive, provocative and wanting sexual abuse.

Therapists may respond to the stories of sexually abused clients by becoming overly protective (Etherington, 2000). They may want to rescue their clients by doing more for them or stretching therapeutic boundaries. By doing so a therapist is in danger of disempowering the client and depreciating their strengths and resources.

Hearing clients' experiences of sexual abuse may trigger memories and thoughts about therapists' own experience of abuse, especially if they have not addressed and processed it (Sanderson, 2013). This may lead to emotional overload and the need to withdraw and disengage from the client as happened in the case described above.

Professional issues

Therapists are often anxious about their skills and abilities to engage competently with clients who have been sexually abused (Stocker, 2014; Yarrow & Churchill, 2009). Lack of knowledge, experience and sensitivity may make a therapist feel overwhelmed or inadequate and have a detrimental effect on the therapeutic process.

Most authors agree on the importance of maintaining good boundaries when working with sexual abuse, but some point out that if boundaries are too rigid they may get in the way of the therapeutic relationship and reinforce clients' beliefs that they are unmotherabe and unlovable (Loris, 1998; C. Sanderson, 2013).

Another professional issue may be therapists' keenness to work on the sexual abuse, as it may be damaging for the therapeutic relationship because trying to speed-up the process may violate the client's sense of autonomy and control (Perlman, 1996).

Gender issues

Therapists' conflicts, beliefs and stereotypes about gender may affect their work with sexually abused clients (Loris, 1998; Little & Hamby, 1999; Sanderson, 2013). In the current climate therapists may sometimes feel 'silenced out of a misguided "political correctness"' (Pearlman & Saakvitne, 1995, p. 191), they may feel uncomfortable to discuss gender issues even though they are an essential part of working with sexual abuse. Male therapists, in particular, may feel 'guilty and ashamed by association' (Pearlman & Saakvitne, 1995, p. 206) and worried that they may experience voyeuristic excitement and sexual arousal while working with female clients who have been abused (Etherington, 2000). The danger is that in seeking to relieve these feelings therapists may try to push them away by projecting them onto the client or by disengaging and distancing themselves from the client.

Traumatic impact on therapists working with sexual abuse

Different authors use different terms – *vicarious traumatisation* (McCann & Pearlman, 1990), *secondary traumatisation* (Pearlman & Saakvitne, 1995), *secondary traumatic stress, compassion fatigue* (Figley, 1995) but there is a general agreement that therapists' abilities to work with clients who have been sexually abused may be negatively affected. Sanderson (2013) warns that emphatic engagement with sexually abused clients may evoke overwhelming emotions like rage, terror and despair or therapists may try to overcompensate their increased vulnerability by feeling grandiose and omnipotent. Another indication of the traumatic impact of working with sexual abuse could be disengaging and distancing from clients, and reduced empathy and compassion (Sanderson, 2013).

Method and methodology

Heuristic inquiry

Willig (2013) argues that it is impossible for a researcher to remain outside of the researched matter. The starting point of this study was the primary researcher's own experience and it led to selecting Moustakas's Heuristic Inquiry (Moustakas, 1990) as an appropriate research method because it not only acknowledges the researcher's involvement but also focuses on his or her lived experience. Heuristic

Inquiry is a process designed to explore and interpret experience by using the self of the researcher (Etherington, 2001).

The heuristic process is based on the following concepts: identifying with the focus of inquiry, self-dialogue, tacit knowing, intuition, indwelling, focusing, and the internal frame of reference. These concepts formed an integral part of the research process, which followed the phases of heuristic research outlined by Moustakas (1990).

Participants

Eight (three male and five female) psychotherapists were selected through a convenience sampling approach and interviewed for the purposes of the study. The respondents were from different sociocultural backgrounds but had all trained and worked in the UK. They were between 32 and 71 years of age and had been working as psychotherapists for between 3 and 17 years. Six of the respondents described their theoretical approaches as 'integrative', two reported they consider themselves to be psychoanalytic/psychodynamic therapists. All participants received detailed information about the research to help them decide whether they would like to take part. By agreeing to participate in the study the participants confirmed they had worked (and continued to work) with sexually abused clients, and they had their own support by way of personal therapy and supervision. They were also offered further support in case they felt distressed after the interview.

Interviews

The interviews were held in the form of unstructured conversations that came to a natural ending between 40 to 60 minutes from the start. The chosen interview method was unstructured to allow a more natural flow of the conversations and a deeper understanding of the interviewees' material but the interviewer offered some prompts and guided questions. The respondents were asked to discuss their experiences of working with sexually abused clients and to give examples of what they thought hindered the therapeutic process.

Data processing

The transcribed interviews were used to identify themes for each participant and ***individual depictions*** were developed. Each individual depiction was sent to the individual it described so they could confirm, correct and/or add information that they felt should be included. The individual depictions were then combined in a ***composite depiction*** that represents the essence of experience for each participant and the group as a whole. Two individual depictions that represent most accurately the themes of the entire group were selected and used to create *exemplary portraits* that demonstrate the essence of the experience of the group in its entirety. The primary researcher then captured and incorporated everything that emerged in a *creative synthesis* in the form of an imaginary letter to Lucy, the client who did not return.

Data analysis and findings

Individual depictions

The primary researcher identified the main themes for each participant and organised them in detailed descriptions to capture the essence of their individual experiences. Due to word count limitations it is not possible to include the individual depictions in this article, however below is an excerpt from the individual depiction of one of the participants:

*** Boris acknowledged a response of guilt and anxiety, and a sense of inadequacy that could get in a way of working with people who have been sexually abused.

'There's guilt, firstly because it would often be men in those roles, but also there's some guilt about not knowing and anxiety around inadequacy, because of not really understanding and the pressure of knowing that it's important ... and for me in this area there's a feeling that I do miss something'

Boris spoke about the challenges of being a male therapist – in addition to the 'low-key shame' related more broadly to his gender he also had to work with clients' anger and aggression towards men.

'I find the whole thing of navigating around gender issues very difficult, and even more so as a male therapist ... One needs to sympathize with where the roots of this are, and there's a long history of women being treated very badly in this world, but at the same time there's something about enduring the clients' attacks and not feeling that those are justified necessarily ... for me it's conflictive, it's tricky. Do I collude with the client's attempt to minimize danger by "castrating" me or do I challenge it and potentially align myself with the aggressor.' ***

The following core themes were used to develop individual depictions for each participant:

Boris: Lack of understanding and empathy; Lack of experience; Sense of inadequacy; Guilt (for being a man; for not being able to fully grasp what is like to be sexually abused); Inability to cope with clients' anger and aggression; Gender issues.

Michelle: Similarities between therapists' and clients' past experiences; Sexual abuse may leave both client and therapist in disarray; Disconnection from own feelings and from the client; Lack of self-awareness; Not maintaining boundaries.

Marina: Complexity of sexual abuse; Forcing clients to discuss their abuse; Not confronting the abuse/colluding with the denial of what happened; Gender issues; Transference issues; Adverse responses to shocking or overwhelming material.

Martin: Shame; Feelings towards the perpetrator; Judgement and inability to empathize; Anxiety around reactions to hearing sexually explicit material.

Natalie: Difficulties to talk about sexual abuse; Rigidly adhering to theoretical models; Rigid boundaries or lack of boundaries; Personal beliefs or stereotypes; Defences when working with clients who have also become perpetrators.

Samuel: Inexperience and nervousness around working with sexual abuse; Inability to maintain boundaries; Feelings and reactions to the presented material, Judgement towards perpetrators; Gender issues.

Sofia: Personal experience of abuse; Difficulties to stay with a client having a flashback and re-experiencing the abuse; Lack of self-awareness; Inability to empathize; Difficulties around discussing sex and sexuality; Failure to maintain boundaries; Anger.

Valerie: Lack of boundaries; Disbelief; Past experiences; Reactions to the presented material, including facial expressions and body language.

Composite depiction

Working with sexual abuse is a challenging experience for both clients and therapists.

When thinking about how therapists may hinder the therapeutic process the participants pointed out that boundaries are very important but sometimes difficult to maintain. Therapists are often protective of sexually abused clients and may want to offer them more support outside the therapeutic relationship, which will be in breach of professional and ethical boundaries. In addition, clients may see such therapists as crossing a line, invading and abusive as their perpetrators.

Maintaining boundaries that are too rigid (i.e. therapists presenting as too closed off or emotionally unavailable) also get in the way as clients may get the impression that therapists are not interested in helping them. Therapists may also use boundaries as a defence against the traumatic material they hear.

Hearing clients speak about being abused provokes different reactions in therapists. They may feel shocked and overwhelmed, angry at the abuser or they may question if what the client is telling them is true. They may feel inadequate and wonder if they are the right therapist for this person. It would be concerning if therapists did not have these reactions because it would mean they probably numbed themselves as a way of defending against the pain and horror of the experience. This leads to inability to be present for the client, to understand and empathise, or as one of the participants described it 'an inability to hop on the client's island and be there for them'. Lack of empathy was named by all participants as one of the biggest blocks when working with sexual abuse.

Getting caught up in therapists' own emotions could also be damaging. Several participants expressed a belief that clients who have been sexually abused are often sensitive and attuned to other people's emotions. They can pick up on their therapists' emotions and decide that it is unsafe to disclose because the therapist seems upset, or shocked, or even disgusted and angry. If a therapist is not self-aware, they can easily project their issues onto clients and re-create situations in which they were ignored, unheard or blamed for what had happened to them.

Therapists' past experiences can become a hindrance to working with people who have been sexually abused especially if they involved neglect and abuse. If a therapist is not able to process these issues, they will not be able to be entirely present for a client who is talking about being abused and there is a risk of painful emotions being triggered by the disclosed material. The participants agreed that when this happens the most common reaction is to withdraw from the client and disconnect as a way of protecting themselves from experiences that feel too harrowing.

Discussing sexual abuse with a client involves talking about sex and sexuality. These are topics that may make therapists feel uncomfortable and anxious. Some of the participants shared their worry that if the material gets too sexually explicit, they may feel too excited and be perceived by the client as voyeuristic and abusive. Others stated that their own difficulties around sex and sexuality might get in the way of the work because they could end up projecting their own issues onto the clients and pushing them to resolve a problem that is not theirs.

The participants also discussed gender issues that may come in the way of working with sexually abused clients. Male therapists spoke about a general sense of guilt about belonging to the gender that is more commonly seen as sexually abusive (even though all participants agreed this is not always the case). They also wondered if they were able to empathise as much as female therapists. Female therapists spoke about aligning themselves more with the victims because historically women have been abused more often than men. Some of the female therapists shared that they have very strong opinions around abuse and sometimes anger towards men in general, and these can get in the way of the work if they do not manage to contain them in the therapy room.

All participants agreed that judgment and imposing their own opinions on the client may hinder the therapeutic process. Therapists would like to believe that they are able to accept their clients and not judge them, but this ability is put to the test especially when working with clients who have become perpetrators themselves. Some participants stated that they would rather not work with such clients as their judgment will come in the way and do more damage than good.

Exemplary portraits

The interviews and the individual depictions of two of the participants that represent most accurately the themes of the entire group were used to developed portraits that exemplify the essence of the experience of the group in its entirety. Below is an excerpt from one of the exemplary portraits:

*** Sofia works exclusively with adult survivors of childhood sexual abuse. She calls herself a *'Survivor therapist'* as she herself was sexually abused in her childhood.

Sofia was in the mental health system for a long time and met many practitioners who not did not help her but made matters worse by not knowing how to work with her, by ignoring and dismissing what she told them and also by being unaware of themselves and projecting their own issues onto her. This is one the reasons Sofia chose to become a psychotherapist and work with sexually abused clients – *'I wanted to be better than all the rubbish people I saw.'*

As a therapist now Sofia believes there are a few things that can come in the way of working with sexual abuse.

Sofia's personal experience is often helpful in her work but she believes that it could come in the way if she was not able to process it in her therapy and supervision. She thinks that lack of self-awareness can be very dangerous not only for the client but for the therapist too.

She is not convinced that therapists get traumatised by hearing clients speak of being sexually abused because she does not feel there can be a comparison between the suffering of the client and the distress of the therapist. However she acknowledges that working with people who have been sexually abused is sometimes very difficult as people talking about their pain could be a trigger to her own pain.

Sofia is aware that sometimes her own experience may have downsides. Because of it she feels protective of her clients and tempted to let boundaries slip despite knowing how important they are. She is tempted to speak to clients not as their therapist but as a survivor of sexual abuse or as an overly protective mother who wants to take them home and make sure they are safe from harm.

She still feels angry at her abuser and is aware that her anger stops her from working with clients who have been sexually abused but have also become perpetrators.

'I really struggle to understand how someone who's been a victim can then create another victim. I completely admire the person who can do this work,

maybe it's something I can do further down the line but at the moment it's a line I draw – so there's a massive block – I just wouldn't do it.' ***

Creative synthesis

The primary researcher's own experience was reflected in the final stage of the Heuristic Inquiry – creative synthesis in the form of a letter to Lucy:

Dear Lucy,

You may not remember me because we met only once but I remember you. I remember how you sat opposite me and told me you felt anxious but seemed absolutely calm. I remember how 5 minutes after the start of our session you told me that you were sexually abused as a child. And then you proceeded to give me all the details – what your uncles did to you, when and how the abuse happened, how many times, for how long, how your mother and grandmother knew but did not help you and how you wished you had a father because maybe he would have saved you.

What you were telling me was horrible but you kept talking flatly and steadily as if you were reading from an invisible book and I could not help wondering how many times you had already said the words 'my uncles did incest on me' and how many times you were failed by the people who heard those words.

Lucy, I am writing this letter to you because I think I failed you too. I do not know why you decided to discontinue therapy after only one session, but I do know that I was not able to be there for you while you were talking about what had happened to you. At first I felt so overwhelmed and shocked by what I heard that I wondered if you were telling me the truth, then I got really angry with your uncles for raping you and the other adults who neglected you and left you alone in your suffering. But what really horrified me was the deadness in your eyes while you were talking. My imagination painted an image of you lying motionless and lifeless waiting for your uncles to finish raping you. It was too much to bear so I retreated to myself – I stopped thinking, I stopped feeling, I heard every word you said clearly but they just seemed to bounce off me. I imagine at that moment I looked just as frozen and lifeless as you. So, there we were – two women, who were in the same room but who could not meet as each one had entered their own dreadful bubble.

For a long time I tried to convince myself that this was just my reaction to the horrible things that happened to you. But something about it kept bothering me, something did not quite make sense. Now I know that what my imagination showed me during our session was not a picture of you but a memory of me lying still, playing dead while waiting for the man who was sexually assaulting me to finish. You see, it is not that I had forgotten about it,

I just put it aside for a long time because I could not face looking at what happened to me. Your story opened an old wound that I have ignored for a long time. It was not as horrible as your wound but my own pain prevented me from being there for you, and putting you first. By being so unaware of myself I unwittingly became like your uncles who ignored your feelings and took care only of their needs and I joined all the people who could have helped you but did not because they were too busy with their own lives.

As a therapist I think there are clients we remember and clients who have a huge impact on us. To me you are one of the latter and I am grateful because what you shared with me made me look at my own story and even though it was painful I think it helped me become a freer person and hopefully a better therapist. But I also feel guilty because I was the one who was supposed to help you. And I am sorry for failing to do so.

Yours

Discussion

The aim of this research was to explore and gain understanding of therapists' experiences of what may hinder therapeutic work with people who have been sexually abused. The starting point was the primary researcher's own experience of feeling inadequate and unhelpful during a session with a sexually abused client and later realising that her own experience of abuse had come in the way.

While there is plenty of existing academic literature on working with sexual abuse, most studies either provide techniques and strategies or discuss the impact this type of work may have on practitioners (Cunningham, 1999; Davies & Frawley, 1994; Figley, 1995; McBride & Markos, 1994; McCann & Pearlman, 1990; Pearlman & Saakvitne, 1995; Sanderson, 1995, 2013; West, 1997). This study was more focused on exploring participants' experiences and opening different possibilities for awareness and insight, rather than giving recommendations and advice on how to work with sexually abused clients. Interestingly none of the participants named vicarious traumatisation as something that they have experienced as an obstacle to working with sexually abused clients (one of the participants mentioned feeling traumatised during a session but she considered it a short-lived experience and did not think it got in the way of her work).

One key theme from previous research (Etherington, 2000; McBride & Markos, 1994; Pearlman & Saakvitne, 1995; Sanderson, 1995) was reiterated in the disclosures of all the participants – the harmful effects of therapists' denial or minimizing of their own abuse history. Questions were raised around adequate ways to train psychotherapists working with sexually abused clients. The shared opinion was that while theoretical information about the nature of sexual abuse and the difficulties our clients face is very helpful, it is far from enough. There is a need for personal exploration of therapists' own experiences, values and believes around sex and sexuality, which can be achieved through supervision and personal therapy and requires a great extent of commitment, sincerity and courage. This has led some of the researchers of the current study to start working on a new project aiming to investigate this finding further and to consider the need for therapists to explore their own sexualities.

Limitations

This study was designed to explore the subjective experience and meaning making of the primary researcher and the participants. It had personal significance for the primary researcher while the participants confirmed in their debrief reports that it was of immense value for them as it allowed for reflection and better understanding of a challenging topic that may be a source of difficulties and discomfort for psychotherapists and their clients.

There are however a few limitations that need to be considered when examining the findings of the study. Heuristic inquiry is a qualitative research method focused on themes and essences of experience and as such it cannot be subjected to quantitative measurements of validity (Moustakas, 1990). In terms of qualitative criteria, credibility and confirmability of the study are based on the judgement of the researchers and achieved through self-validation (through creative synthesis) and participant verifications (through sending the individual depictions to each participant and requesting their confirmation that the depictions were accurate). The researchers view the findings of the study as valuable and validating the experience of each participant but are also aware that these are unique individual experiences that may not be universal, which may prove the study difficult to be replicated and scrutinised.

Another limitation of the study is the number and the broad selection criteria of the participants. At the start of the research process the researchers aimed for a higher number of participants and left the inclusion criteria deliberately broad to ensure more participants. After completion, however, the researchers believe that a smaller number and a less diverse group of participants may have facilitated deeper understanding of each individual experience.

Conclusion

The findings of the current study were mostly consistent with existing academic literature, but the research was focused on more specific examples and more in-depth exploration of therapists' experiences. The participants were able to discuss challenges and difficulties in their work with sexually abused clients, and to look at how their personal stories affected the therapeutic process. The study contains subtle nuances and levels of honest self-exploration that according to the researchers are not clearly demonstrated in previous studies. Each individual added something uniquely personal and yet essential to the overall significance of the study.

Disclosure statement

No potential conflict of interest was reported by the author(s).

References

Braun, V., & Clarke, V. (2006). Using thematic analysis in psychology. *Qualitative Research in Psychology*, 3(2), 77–101. https://doi.org/10.1191/1478088706qp063oa

Cunningham, M. (1999). The impact of sexual abuse treatment on the social work clinician. *Child & Adolescent Social Work Journal, 16*(4), 277–290. https://doi.org/10.1023/A:1022334911833

Davies, J. M., & Frawley, M. G. (1994). *Treating the adult survivor of childhood sexual abuse.* Basic Books.

Etherington, K. (2000). Supervising counsellors who work with survivors of childhood sexual abuse. *Counselling Psychology Quarterly, 13*(4), 377–389. https://doi.org/10.1080/713658497

Etherington, K. (2001). Writing qualitative research — A gathering of selves. *Counselling and Psychotherapy Research, 1*(2), 2. https://doi.org/10.1080/14733140112331385158

Figley, C. R. (1995). *Compassion fatigue: Coping with secondary traumatic disorder in those who treat the traumatized.* Brunner/Mazel.

Little, L., & Hamby, S. (1999). Gender differences in sexual abuse outcomes and recovery experiences: A survey of therapist-survivors. *Professional Psychology: Research and Practice, 30*(4), 378–385. https://doi.org/10.1037/0735-7028.30.4.378

Loris, M. C. (1998). A case of "Loving Hate. *Journal of Child Sexual Abuse: Research, Treatment & Program Innovations for Victims, Survivors & Offenders, 7*(1), 65–80. https://doi.org/10.1300/J070v07n01_05

McBride, M., & Markos, P. (1994). Sources of difficulty in counselling sexual abuse victims and survivors. *Canadian Journal of Counselling, 28*(1), 83–99. https://cjc-rcc.ucalgary.ca/article/view/58495

McCann, I. L., & Pearlman, L. A. (1990). Vicarious traumatisation: A framework for understanding the psychological effects of working with victims. *Journal of Traumatic Stress, (3)*(1), 131–149. https://doi.org/10.1007/BF00975140

Moustakas, C. (1990). *Heuristic research, design, methodology and applications.* Sage Publications.

Pearlman, L. A., & Saakvitne, K. W. (1995). *Trauma and the therapist: Countertransference and vicarious traumatization in psychotherapy with incest survivors.* Norton.

Perlman, S. D. (1996). 'Reality' and countertransference in the treatment of sexual abuse patients: The false memory controversy. *Journal of the American Academy of Psychoanalysis, 24*(1), 115–135. https://doi.org/10.1521/jaap.1.1996.24.1.115

Sanderson, C. (1995). *Counselling adult survivors of child sexual abuse.* Jessica Kingsley Publishers.

Sanderson, C. (2013). *Counselling skills for working with trauma: Healing from child sexual abuse, sexual violence and domestic abuse.* Jessica Kingsley Publishers.

Stocker, P. (2014). Into the labyrinth: A case study of a therapist's journey with and adult survivor of childhood abuse. *International Journal of Integrative Psychotherapy, 5*(1), 1–20. https://www.integrative-journal.com/index.php/ijip/article/view/93

West, J. (1997). Caring for ourselves: The impact of working with abused children. *Child Abuse Review, 6*(4), 291–297. https://doi.org/10.1002/(SICI)1099-0852(199710)6:4<291::AID-CAR345>3.0.CO;2-G

Willig, C. (2013). *Introducing qualitative research in psychology.* Open University Press.

Yarrow, C., & Churchill, S. (2009). Counsellors' and psychologists' experience of working with male survivors of sexual trauma: A pilot study. *Counselling Psychology Quarterly, 22*(2), 267–277. https://doi.org/10.1080/09515070903171926

Maculate conceptions

Manu Bazzano

ABSTRACT
A refreshing ambivalence at the heart of psychoanalysis makes it straddle both modernist and poststructuralist narratives, shielding it from its penchant for universalism. Similarly, when phenomenological and heuristic styles of research are held lightly and critically, and no longer constricted by subjectivism and a philosophy of consciousness, they can be more effective in navigating the intricacies of human experience and open the exploration to postqualitative investigation.

Conquest and adventure

A clear-cut distinction is often assumed between modernism and postmodernism, each of them represented as standing for something specific:

reliance on grand narratives in the case of modernism; perspectivism, or even 'relativism', in the case of post-modernism. This assumption, however, may betray an inherently modernist narrative (Jameson, 2019). While we are busy diagnosing the end of ideology and the dawn of an age of difference, we may unwittingly affirm ideology in its most powerful guise – hidden, pervasive, heralding the triumph of pluralism-as-consumer-choice, of perspectivism as anything-goes-philosophy, and affirming, rather alarmingly, via a generic postmodernist stance, the ideology of 'the market', of neoliberalism and of what has been recently called *vectoralism* (Wark, 2019).

These reflections came up when reading the seemingly optimistic embracing of postmodernism in Onel Brook's paper 'Looking Like a Foreigner: foreignness, conformity and compliance in psychoanalysis', where the reader is invited to understand postmodernism as 'a name for an attempt to escape from and think about … assumptions and convictions', or as an effort 'to come to terms with the "limits and limitations" of modernism' as a manner of staying with 'doubts, uncertainties and anxieties' (Brooks). This invitation to think critically and deconstruct the universalizing axioms inherent in psychoanalysis is attuned to the 'critical existential-analytic psychotherapies' project sketched in the Editorial (Loewenthal, 2020). It is analogous to the critique found in Critical Theory, but without the invaluable caveat found in the latter: critique of reason does not entail abdication to the irrationality and closeted-theology found, for instance, in Heidegger and in those 'postmodern' stances promoting a jargon of authenticity (Adorno, 1964/2002). We do not find critique of reason *tout court* but trenchant critique of reason's chief enemy, i.e., *rationalization* (Adorno & Horkheimer, 1944/1997). For Adorno and Horkheimer, what often passes for reason is not the clearing of clouds heralded by the *Aufklärung*/Enlightenment, nor the maturity of thought praised by Kant, but its opposite, *degeneration* of reason, which in my view is precisely what a generic postmodern stance has promoted and substantiated.

But what *is* postmodernism? Can its troubled, many-sided and sedimented histories since Lyotard's book in the late nineteen seventiess (Lyotard, 1979/1984) be condensed in one formula? Is the postmodern really continuous with the preoccupations highlighted by 'Sophocles through to Kierkegaard, Nietzsche and Wittgenstein' (Brooks)? And what is the connection, if any, between postmodernism and deconstruction, or postmodernism and poststructuralism?

Brooks' paper presents telling and convincing illustrations from clinical practice and everyday experience; it mounts an engaging critique of the universalizing, tendencies in psychoanalysis, seen as part and parcel of a generalized 'modernist' project which assumes western culture's epistemological superiority against the alleged credulity of cultures arrogantly perceived as subaltern and even accursed. I'll leave aside the argument that modernism in art, literature, and culture has given birth to a tidal wave of experimentation, innovation and daring of the sort our profoundly acquiescent age cannot even dream of. Brooks's argument is convincing when it alerts us to the alarming levels of conformity and compliance present in psychoanalytic training (and, I would add, in most psychotherapy trainings)

It is not really possible, as Brooks offers to nominally do in passing, to dismiss Freud's claim, in a letter to Wilhelm Fliess, of 'not being a man of science, not an observer, not an experimenter, not a thinker [but] by temperament, nothing but a conquistador' (as cited in Winter, 1999:341 n). On the contrary, Freud's claim must be accurately read and understood, and Brooks's invitation to do so is timely. The term 'conquistador' rings alarm bells, insinuating blatant similarity, allegiance and complicity with the proficient criminal pillaging perpetrated by Spanish and Portuguese plunderers and mercenaries who exploited human and natural resources between the sixteenth and eighteenth centuries.. It would have been good, however, *not* to omit, as Brooks does, the very next thing Freud writes in his letter. He says 'I am by temperament nothing but a conquistador – an *adventurer*, if you want it translated' (Winter, 199:341 n). Freud is conquistador *and* adventurer, colonizer *and* dissenter, bringing forth a perspective/praxis that is both conventional *and* subversive, both loyal to and discontented with civilization.

One way to understand the dichotomy between conquest and adventure is intrapsychic. Take, for instance, Freud's gnomic dictum *where it was, there I shall be*. With psychodynamic therapists now busy, in our times of 'hypertrophied consciousness' (Bollas, 2007, p. 81), with the delusional endeavour of making the unconscious conscious, the dictum may be read as the attempt by an essentially reactive, 'symptomatic' faculty, i.e., consciousness, to conquer the multiplicity of *psyche* and the complexity of becoming within which it is embedded. Conversely, a reading that were to take poststructuralism and deconstruction to heart may edit Freud's motto to *where it was, there others shall be*, a notion that is inspired by the remarkable work of J. Laplanche (1989, 1998, 1996).

'*I* shall be' may have set off the therapy enterprise on the wrong foot, establishing the primacy of the self, leading us to believe that the unknown can be known, that the enigma of psychic life can be translated, and what is other can be reduced to the same. Despite their official protestations, all therapeutic approaches followed suit, via appeals to 'evidence-based' claims, the wild-goose chase for 'authenticity', or the fashionable delusions of integration and regulation. '*Others* shall be' may on the other hand help us reveal the essential *heteronomy* present in the heart of autonomy (M. Bazzano, 2020b), the profound influences of concrete others in our life, whether alive or dead

Brooks's critique of Freud, though not new, is still urgent; it applies to psychotherapy as a whole and the 'various gurus' (Loewenthal, 2020) on which current therapy trainings are based. Freud emerges in Brooks's paper as the advocate of a methodology of conquest upholding a monolithic view of his creation, with obvious and highly questionable blind spots in relation to race, culture, class and gender – views which then predictably fossilized through tedious internecine and sectarian wars within the psychoanalytic church. At the same time, the other aspect, equally present in Freud, e.g., psychotherapy as experimentation and adventure (M. Bazzano, 2019a; Russell, 2017) is conspicuously absent from the investigation. One immediate association to Freud as adventurer relates to what Lacan heard *viva voce* from Jung:

> Thus Freud's words to Jung – I have it from Jung's own mouth – when, on an invitation from Clark University, they arrived in New York harbour and caught their first glimpse of the famous statue illuminating the universe, 'They don't realize we're bringing them the plague,' are attributed to him as confirmation of a hubris whose antiphrasis and gloom do not extinguish their troubled brightness. To catch their author in its trap, Nemesis had only to take him at his word. We could be justified in fearing that Nemesis has added a first-class return ticket".. (Lacan, 1977, p. 116)

'They don't realize we're bringing them the plague' are, arguably, not the words of someone carrying the tables of the law to the superstitious, but those of a subversive adventurer instilling the Schopenhauerian worm of perplexity and pessimism in a societal fabric built on blind positivity and positivism (the 'American dream'). The anecdotal statement chimes with the first generalized reception of psychoanalysis in the US. Jacqueline Rose (2011) reminds us of the story of the American woman who, during a lecture by Ernest Jones on dreams, objected that Jones could speak only for Austrians; in her case, as with her fellow Americans, all dreams were positive and altruistic.

'They don't realize we're bringing them the plague' are the words of a *European*, of someone who, schooled in European high culture, was deeply sceptical of the commercialism and superficiality of the official American way of life. It is true, as Brooks writes, that Europe has 'plundered, massacred, enslaved and dominated the foreign others it has encountered'. It is also true, if one is to believe Adorno (1951/2005) and Said (1979), that at the heart of European high culture there was (is) that *transcendental homelessness* that became painfully tangible through the horrors of the twentieth century. One could argue that the very notion of 'Europe' is specious: not only does Europe have deep roots in the East and the Middle East (Said, 1979), but the flowering of European culture is itself the product of exiles (Adorno, 1951/2005; M. Bazzano, 2006, 2012), rather than the straightforward manifestation of an imaginary European identity. In Freud's case, the rabid anti-Semitic prejudice he was subjected to, in France and elsewhere, also reminds us of the way in which his creation was inextricably associated with otherness and the attendant fears of contamination.

There is in my view one crucial aspect (half-concealed and barely articulated in Freud; conspicuously absent from current psychotherapeutic discourse) – which would make psychoanalysis immediately relevant to any project aspiring to be post-existential. This is Freud's brief, tentative admission of the *primacy of the other* present in his discarded theory of seduction and in his unachieved Copernican revolution (J. Laplanche, 1996).

Primacy of the other runs parallel in poststructuralism and deconstruction to a *decentering of the self*. There is no serious move away in psychotherapy from grand 'modernist' narratives without instituting these two crucial aspects: primacy of the other, decentering of the self. Without these, all talk of 'post-existential' critical-analytic psychotherapies is just that: empty talk, hazardously lenient to the platitudes of a facile and utterly vacuous 'pluralistic' approach to psychotherapy. Equally, there is no significant shift away from the modernist, biological pieties of Attachment Theory (a universalized grand narrative if there ever was one, supinely accepted by *all* psychotherapies) without a thoroughgoing reinstatement of the primacy of the other and a decentering of the self (M. Bazzano, 2020a).

I would add to the mix a third element: *ontology of actuality*, a concept alive in Critical Theory, one that Foucault (1983) rightly saw as necessary antidote to the inherent trappings of that philosophy of consciousness (Dews, 1986) within whose precincts existential phenomenological therapies seem to enjoy wallowing. Bluntly put: by focusing on the deed rather than the doer, on history rather than an imaginary fall from being, on situational, progressive and subversive action rather than abstract ontological ethical principles, we may at least avoid varnishing the same old *cogito*. Actuality, history and at times even contingency are blissfully and ignorantly absent from existential phenomenological therapy, an approach that would have greatly benefited from Hegel, in whose writings the ontology of actuality figures prominently:

> An individual cannot know what he is until he has made himself a reality through action. However, this seems to imply that he cannot determine the end of his action until he has carried it out; but at the same time, since he is a conscious individual, he must have the action in front of him beforehand as entirely his own, i.e. as an end. (Hegel, 1977, p. 240)

Good players and bad players

Actuality, deed, and more specifically *gesture* (and its relation to language) are at the heart of Julia Cayne's investigation in 'Language as Gesture in Merleau-Ponty: Some implications for method in therapeutic practice and research'. Vividly recounted through the vignette of playing with grandchildren, the paper initially presents a stimulating and refreshing take on Winnicott, his notion of play, its connection to creativity and the spontaneous gesture. Winnicott valued *play* as an activity that is not dissimilar from being itself, as 'a type of doing that being is' (Russell, 2017, p. 105). Play may also be understood, *contra* the dominant view, as an expansive and generous notion of 'wellbeing' that far exceeds the miserly view of mental health currently in vogue, as mere avoidance of illness. This is a reactive notion – the stance of a *bad player*. What makes a bad player? A calculating stance, playing in order to win, arbitrarily assigning purpose, unity, and meaning to an unfathomable existence, a pervasive fear of becoming and its intrinsic innocence, the latter understood as 'the truth of multiplicity' (Deleuze, 1962/2006, p. 21). What makes a *good player*? Well, for one thing, disposing of notions of loss and gain when throwing the dice; actively accepting the limitations of our Promethean will to control, measure, and quantify everything under the sun. Can then a phenomenologist be a good player? Yes, if she no longer sees phenomenology as mere prelude and propaedeutic to the study of abstractions such as 'Being', but is capable of actively partaking in the play of multiplicity. A phenomenologist can be a good player if he/she is able to appreciate *phenomena* as semblance/emergence rather than 'mere' appearance, without assuming the existence of *noumena*, essences, or 'the things themselves'. But this would require a momentous shift; it would involve abandoning notions of purpose, evolution and *telos*; it would involve 'substituting the venerable old pair of probability/finality with the Dionysian pairs of chance/necessity and chance/destiny' (M. Bazzano, 2019a, p. 20).

Simplistically put, it would also involve, I suspect, holding (very) lightly the structuralist view of language common to Saussure and early Lacan and move the investigation further, spurred by that openness to difference already present in Merleau-Ponty who, as I read him, understood language less as a sum of signs and more as an orderly way to single out each sign from another, thus weaving a *multi*verse, never bypassing the importance of subjective difference in the name of universality. This essential move into difference – and differentialism – is greatly hindered, as Cayne rightly points out, by seeing qualitative phenomenological research 'as stemming from the dominant discourse around a positivist paradigm'. Is the researcher's need to respond to the inevitable 'disorientation and uncertainty' of one's 'engagement' and 'intermingling with others' doomed to be narrowed down to cosily dim and wearisome positivist narratives? Sadly, the general trend in psychotherapy trainings appears to confirm this. Perhaps a shred of hope in a landscape dominated by obsessive measurement disorder (Bazzano, 2020c) may exist via the first attempts towards developing postqualitative research. Despite being very tentative and sporadic, these significantly gesture towards, among other creative uncertainties and disorientations, the unreliability and insubstantiality of the subject.

The notion of language as gesture cuts through the solipsism of self-reflection; it presents us with a language able to retrieve those voices that rationalization cannot hear, making possible a 'remembrance of nature within the subject' (Adorno & Horkheimer, 1944/2003, p. 32). From its initial babbling and its onomatopoeic beginnings language *sings the world*, expressing an emotional essence that resonates in the human *weatherscape* (Stern, 1985, 1992). Having capitalized on Merleau-Ponty's work and the notion of language-as-gesture, the next stage of an exploration of language which were to embrace poststructuralism involves absorbing Artaud's (and Deleuze & Guattari's) notion of the *body without organs* (Artaud, 1958/1976; Deleuze & Guattari, 1972/1982), describing a world of intensities-in-motion, a primal order of language that is already there before the infant can begin to grasp words and sentences, the perception of a voice endowed with the dimensions of language but not its meanings (Deleuze, 1969/2004). It also provokes phenomenologists, habitually confined by the intrinsic limitation of their ideology to an aseptic notion of experience as a contemplative, irremediably Kantian connection with the world, to the tragic and potentially emancipatory meaning of experience as liberation from a body-subject that is subjected to interpellation (Althusser, 2005) and the surveillance and cataloguing of medicine and biology (Foucault, 2008). It is this more overtly political aspect of experience – politics of the gesture as much as politics of experience – that may afford the researcher with a glimpse of a more objective *Stimmung* outside the Cartesian cocoon within which existential phenomenology remains arguably trapped. This, rather than appeals to 'the body', a term which cannot itself 'escape the reproach of reification' (Jameson, 2013, p. 31). This, rather than Gaston Bachelard's psychoanalysis of the elements and its attendant anthropomorphism.

The private screech of wild birds

It is hard to resist the romantic notion that imagines 'experience' to be raw, immaculate, full of richly entwined complexities which elude us because we have been so fatally obstructed by synthetic methods and theories. It is even harder when the theories/methods in question are gimmicky, put in place in order to subtly coerce researchers into complying with the various transactions that keep that commercial enterprise going that we grandly call 'university'. And it is nearly impossible to resist the seductive image of 'screeching wild birds' removed to an 'aviary' and not wanting to preserve and defend their wildness, which is the wildness of sensual meaning against the dullness and imposition of mechanical theory and evidence-based conformity.

All the same, the notion that by 'being phenomenological we are less likely' to become 'caught up' (McSherry, Loewenthal and Cayne, in 'The private life of meaning – some implications for psychotherapy and psychotherapeutic research') in the constrictions of a research method, must be resisted. The view of phenomenology as a method and a theory which apparently escapes '"given" meanings' and is more in touch with the 'contextual origin [of] sensual meaning' (ibid) is at best naive, and at worst delusional. If anything, the 'method' makes us painfully aware of our inevitable biases and (equally inevitable) estrangement from supposedly raw and immaculate sensual meaning. This error, I suspect, is inbuilt in the apparatus assembled by Husserl's followers, old and new, with its unwavering Cartesian itch towards the so-called 'things themselves', setting back the phenomenological endeavour to Kantian psychology. It would be incongruous for any self-styled 'post-phenomenologist' to advocate the undoing of all 'layers of knowledge and metaphysics and [arriving at] the final unveiling of a natural substratum' (Bazzano, 2019a, p. 103). From Nietzsche – and from post-structuralism – we have learned that there is no natural substratum; that the 'naked' body is not the ultimate ground; that there is no 'ground', ultimate or not. What we can hope for is to weave a garment that better fits, rather than constrains and distorts, the contours of the human body.

Nevertheless, McSherry, Loewenthal and Cayne make a convincingly subjectivist defense of the art of healing. The context – the mental nursing milieu – and the theoretical frame – Amedeo Giorgi's own singular adaptation of Husserlian methodologies – are the background on which their argument is built. They are politely critical of Giorgi's translation of the research participants' words 'into *transformed meaning units* of accepted psychological language' (emphasis in the original). They see this process of translation (rightly, in my view) as losing an essential component of phenomenology: the loss of the 'sensual', understood as the subjective landscape in the name of obeisance to '"given" psychological meanings'. Translating is traducing; translating is betraying; it is oversimplification, banalization, and inevitable repression of subjective experience. What McSherry, Loewenthal and Cayne do not consider is that what is commonly understood as 'subjective experience' is in turn a 'meaning unit', a 'given'. The subjective sphere is itself an oversimplification, an essentially repressive banalization of *affect* and of pre-subjective subjectivities (Combes, 2013). I see this as a failing that is constitutive of Husserlian phenomenology. It is certainly a *creative* failing, strategically valuable in shielding the 'absolute *solitude* of the *existent* in its *existence*' (Derrida, 1967/2005, p. 110) from the onslaught of data and those mechanical generalities that are now the staple of neoliberal therapy training and 'research'. But it is a failing all the same, for it hampers the enquiry through an *a priori* form of sensibility and a *private logic*, Adler would say (Ansbacher & Ansbacher, 1964), that is inimical to common sense, a.k.a. shared wisdom. Granted, this criticism could be pointedly applied to 'early' Husserl, a thinker still arguably enthralled by both Descartes and, to a certain degree Kant. There appears to be in the Husserl's late writings a recognition of the pre-reflective, intersubjective realm of 'Lebenswelt'.

Subjectivism breeds objectivism; how to steer clear of this epistemological trap? One way out is offered by Gilbert Simondon, who in *L'individuation psychique et collective* (Simondon, 1989) writes:

> If knowledge rediscovers the lines that allow for interpreting the world according to stable laws, it is not because there exist in the subject a priori forms of sensibility, whose coherence with brute facts coming from the world would be inexplicable; it is because being as subject and being as object arise from the same primitive reality, and the thought that now appears to institute an inexplicable relation between object and subject in fact prolongs this initial individuation; the *conditions of possibility* of knowledge are in fact the *causes of existence* of the individuated being (cited in Combes, 2013: 7-8, emphasis in the original).

The task of 'post-phenomenology' is to go beyond hermeneutics, a science which, championed by Husserl and glorified by Heidegger, entirely relies on givens, 'on a *prior pre-comprehension* or proto-comprehension' (J. Laplanche, 1996:7, emphasis added), or on notions such as *habitus* and the 'abidingly' arché of the 'Ego' (Husserl, 1981, p. 66). McSherry, Loewenthal and Cayne cogently call into question the imposition of 'theoretical [and] evidence-based ideas'; they importantly remind us of asymmetry and openness but the investigation does not go far enough into questioning the very nature of what they call a 'sensual (private and unfolding) meaning'. We may need to listen again to the screeches of those wild birds clamouring through the trees.

How to kill a frog

Elizabeth Nicholl as lead author in 'Finding my voice: Telling stories with heuristic self-search inquiry' reminds us of the intrinsic value of subjective experience over and above the stigmatizations and objectifications of (often crude applications of) science. Tacit knowledge, self-discovery and self-dialogue are (alongside other aspects of first-person heuristic inquiry) paramount in (self-) understanding the first person experience of those diagnosed with 'schizophrenia'. Heuristic inquiry – or for that matter phenomenological research – are not inimical to science but only, I would argue, to naive *scientism*, i.e. the transforming of scientific discourse 'into a vast reservoir of metaphors or "models" for the hard-pressed theoretician' (Derrida, 1974, p. 62). The task in (Merleau-Pontian) phenomenology is not to abandon science but momentarily *forswearing* it (Merleau-Ponty, 1964) by comparing it with other facets of human experience of which science is but one aspect. In the past (Bazzano, 2011), I have personally found one potential way out of an almost inevitable and sterile opposition between 'science' and 'heuristic' experience through the findings of *neuro-phenomenology*, a method championed by Chilean scientist Francisco Varela. A key method consists in combining *first-person report* with *third-person description*.

> Unlike the allegedly 'neutral' and 'objective' procedures used in mainstream science, this time the person experiencing and observing a particular phenomenon is fully in the picture, rather than left out. However, the investigation does not stop here; if it did, the enquiry would be merely subjective. Instead, the first-person account is described and further clarified by a third person description of the same phenomenon. (Bazzano, 2011, p. 22)

The process sparks a dynamic feedback which takes the enquiry beyond both mere subjectivity and the objectivism of hard science. The above is not only compatible with both Moustakas' (1990) formidable template and with Sela-Smith's (2002) update and critique of the former; it also offers one possible way out of a defensive subjectivist position.

At the same time, for some of us the time has come to exit not only the stifling dwelling of quantitative research and its attendant reliance on the McNamara fallacy (Yankelovich, 1972), but also the formulaic vagaries of qualitative research whose touchy-feely lingo barely hides what truly runs the show: *algorithms, impact factor*, tribal waving of shibboleths ('I'm being truly person-centred, I have mentioned the word "empathy" ten times') and so forth. A five-year stint as editor of a humanistic psychotherapy journal has cured me of any illusion on that front. What to do? One interesting field of investigation is currently offered by postqualitative research (Le Grange, 2018). Still in its infancy and despite possible misgivings (e.g., excessive reliance on the tenets of posthumanism), the latter offers a prospective way out of the stiffness of quantitative research and the indulgent preciousness of qualitative research. Among others, its strong points are, as I see it: (a) deconstruction and critical re-evaluation of the subject/researcher to include the nonhuman in the field of an awareness not bound by a philosophy of consciousness; (b) due attention paid to ongoing decolonial conversations and to the findings of poststructuralism.

The narrator/researcher is an unreliable subject, and one deconstructing means may be offered by humour – something which, as Patricia Talens remind us in her rather humourless paper, can help 'facilitate relational desires which may not feel acceptable or appropriate to vocalise within the therapeutic relationship'. For not only is it impossible to dissect humour without killing it, as one would a frog; it may also be unworkable to write about it in an academic paper. In deciding to do so, we join the *tradition* from Plato to Freud and also find that in the therapy room humour may have remedial properties and come in handy when handling totemic subjects like sex and death. When, that is, humour is not superiorly dispatched as defense, catalogued as coping mechanism, or patronized as social lubricant.

Interestingly, Bergson, Bataille, and Plessner are conspicuously absent from the discussion. All three had many interesting things to say on the subject, and from a *counter-traditional stance*. For Helmut Plessner (1970), one of the exponents, with Max Scheler and others, of *philosophical anthropology*, 'the human position' is seen as inherently 'eccentric' (p 36). We do not coincide with ourselves but inhabit a gap between a physical and a psychological dimension. This is where laughter stems from – from our originary inauthenticity (M. Bazzano, 2012; Critchley, 2008)

Embedded in the animal kingdom, we have deliberately placed ourselves outside it via an act of *Abgehobenheit*, or apartness. In this peculiarly human situation of 'mediated immediacy', the human being experiences herself *as* and *within* a thing, a thing differentiating itself from all other things because she is herself that thing. She finds herself sustained and surrounded by something that keeps resisting her. To fully recognize this condition liberates us from the obligation to tag along the latest epistemologies and invites us to accept the ambivalence between presence and apartness, proximity and remoteness, objectivity and subjectivity. But this acceptance implies an exit from the edifice of the tradition, to which Plato, Freud and Husserlian/Heideggerian phenomenology firmly belong, and embracing instead the *counter-tradition* (Bazzano & Webb, 2016).

Think again

Iana Trichkova, Del Loewenthal, Betty Bertrand and Cath Altson's paper, 'What gets in the way of working with clients who have been sexually abused' stopped me in my tracks. Not only because of the shocking, disturbing and painful content directly evoking a range of feelings within me. Not only because of the crystal-clear clarity, competence and attention to detail with which the article is written. It is also a great example of the effectiveness of heuristic inquiry when it is done properly. The latter point forces me to rethink my own stance around research. My eagerness to abandon qualitative research methods has justifiably fed on years of reading and assessing formulaic, box-ticking exercises that pay lip-service to 'experience', 'felt-sense', 'empathic attunement' while promoting a conformist agenda that in its convenient and at times cynical adoption of humane/humanistic lingo is as far removed from the tragic joys and tribulations often at the heart of the subject being explored. This is eerily similar to parody: using right-brain style of speech to advance left-brain agendas. Or, closer to the topic discussed by Trichkova et al., it reminds me of the way some of us men have for years paid lip-service to feminism, all the while displaying a peculiar blindness to women's subjectivities (M. Bazzano, 2019b).

What gets in the way of working with clients who suffered sexual abuse? Well, virtually everything, from feeling overwhelmed to experiencing 'anger, repulsion, and hatred, fear and helplessness, confusion, puzzlement, even shock and horror, grief and sadness, anxiety, guilt and shame'. What responses are unhelpful? Most of the usual ones: from questioning the content to voyeuristic interest, to the usual array of (nevertheless useful) countertransferential responses. All but *one* response are a long way from being even adequate. The heart of Trichkova et al.'s paper is the letter to their client. This is what presents us with an incredible mixture of disarming honesty, profound insight/hindsight, appropriate personal disclosure, and thorough self-reflection. It *shows* directly – rather than merely telling – what heuristic research can accomplish. In questioning the researcher's own responses and the author's general sense of self, it also presents me with a fitting reminder, at the conclusion of this brief foray, that alongside the critique of heuristic and phenomenological styles of research I have expressed throughout this piece, there is room for discovering anew their inherent and implicit value.

Disclosure statement

No potential conflict of interest was reported by the author(s).

References

Adorno, T. (1951/2005). *Minima moralia: reflections on damaged life*. Verso.
Adorno, T. (1964/2002). *The jargon of authenticity*. Routledge.
Adorno, T., & Horkheimer, W. (1944/1997). *Dialectic of enlightenment*. London: Verso.
Adorno, T., & Horkheimer, M. (1944/2003). *Dialectic of enlightenment: philosophical fragments*. Stanford University Press.
Althusser, L. (2005). *For marx*. Verso.
Ansbacher, H. L., & Ansbacher, R. R. (1964). *The individual psychology of alfred adler*. Harper Perennial.

Artaud, A. (1958/1976). *Selected writings*. (S. Sontag, Edited by). Berkeley University Press.
Bazzano, M. (2006). *Buddha is dead: nietzsche and the dawn of European zen*. Sussex Academic Press.
Bazzano, M. (2011). Reclaiming Diagnosis. *Therapy Today*, November, 21–23. www.manubazzano.com/uploads/Reclaiming%20Diagnosis.pdf
Bazzano, M. (2012). *Spectre of the stranger: towards a phenomenology of hospitality*. Sussex Academic Press.
Bazzano, M. (2019a). *Nietzsche and Psychotherapy*. Routledge.
Bazzano, M. (2019b, November). Sons of our Fathers. *Therapy Today*, *20*(9), 24–27. https://www.bacp.co.uk/bacp-journals/therapy-today/2019/november-2019/sons-of-our-fathers/
Bazzano, M. (2020a). *Subversion therapy: Promoting intelligence, affect and rebellion in the age of neoliberal stupidity*. Seminar, University of Brighton, April 18.
Bazzano, M. (2020b). *Where it was, others shall be: Desire, otherness, and the alien inside*. Society of existential analysis seminar, Birkbeck University, February 8.
Bazzano, M. (2020c). The skin is faster than the word. *Existential Analysis*, *31.1*, 53–64. www.manubazzano.com/uploads/SkinFasterThanWord.pdf
Bazzano, M., & Webb, J. (2016). *Therapy and the counter-tradition: the edge of philosophy*. Routledge.
Bollas, C. (2007). *The freudian moment*. London: Karnac.
Combes, M. (2013). *Gilbert simondon and the philosophy of the transindividual*. M.I.T.
Critchley, S. (2008). *Infinitely demanding*. Verso.
Deleuze, G. (1962/2006). *Nietzsche and Philosophy*. Continuum.
Deleuze, G. (1969/2004). *The logic of sense*. Continuum.
Deleuze, G., & Guattari, F. (1972/1982). *Anti-oedipus: capitalism and schizophrenia*. University of Minnesota Press.
Derrida, J. (1967/2005). *Writing and difference*. Routledge.
Derrida, J. (1974). White mythology: metaphor in the text of philosophy. In Bruce Holsinger (Ed.), *New literary history* (Vol. 6.1). John Hopkins University Press, 5–74.
Dews, P. (1986). Adorno, post-structuralism and the critique of identity. *New Left Review I*, no. 157, 28–44.
Foucault, M. (1983). Structuralism and post-structuralism: an interview with michel foucault. *Telos*, 55, 200.
Foucault, M. (2008). *The birth of biopolitics: lectures at the collège de france, 1978-1979*. Palgrave MacMillan.
Hegel, G. W. F. (1977). *Phenomenology of spirit*. Oxford University Press.
Husserl, E. (1981). *Shorter works*. Notre Dame, IN: University of Notre Dame Press.
Jameson, F. (2013). *The antinomies of realism*. Verso.
Jameson, F. (2019). *Allegory and ideology*. Verso.
Lacan, J. (1977). *Écrits: A Selection*. New York.
Laplanche, J. (1989). *New foundations for psychoanalysis*. Blackwell.
Laplanche, J. (1996). Psychoanalysis as anti-hermeneutics. *Radical Philosophy*, no. 79 (September/October), 7–12.
Laplanche, J. (1998). *Essays on Otherness*. Routledge.
Le Grange, L. (2018). What is postqualitative research? *South African Journal of Higher Education*, *32*(5), 1-14.

Loewenthal, D. (2020). editorial: critical existential-analytic psychotherapies: some implications for practices, theories and research. *European Journal of Psychotherapy and Counselling.*

Lyotard, F. (1979/1984) *The postmodern condition: a report on knowledge.* Manchester university press.

Moustakas, C. (1990). *Heuristic Research: Design, Methodology and Application.* Sage.

Plessner, H. (1970). *Laughing and crying: a study of the limits of human behavior.* Northwestern University Press.

Rose, J. (2011). *Proust among the nations: from dreyfus to the middle east.* Chicago University Press.

Russell, J. (2017). *Nietzsche and the clinic: psychoanalysis, philosophy, metaphysics.* Karnac.

Said, E. W. (1979). *Reflections on exiles and other literary and cultural essays.* London: Granta.

Sela-Smith, S. (2002). *Heuristic Research: A Review and Critique of Moustakas's Method Journal of Humanistic Psychology,* 4293, 53–88.

Simondon, G. (1989). *L'individuation psychique et collective.* Aubier.

Stern, D. (1985). *The Interpersonal World of the Infant.* Basic Books.

Stern, D. (1992). *Diary of a baby: what your child sees, feels, and experiences.* Basic Books.

Wark, M. (2019). *Capital is Dead: Is this Something Worse?* Verso.

Winter, S. (1999). *Freud and the institution of psychoanalytic knowledge.* Stanford University Press.

Yankelovich, D. (1972). *Corporate priorities: A continuing study of the new demands on business.* D. Yankelovich Inc.

The pictures you paint in the stories you tell, a response

Laura Chernaik

ABSTRACT
This paper is a phenomenological and psychoanalytical response to a set of papers. As a psychoanalyst, philosopher, and intellectual historian, I am interested in 'intention' in the phenomenological sense, that is, how someone both reaches out to and shapes their world. How does our thinking in this phenomenological way affect our doing of empirical research? How does it affect our psychoanalytical practice? I argue for approaching this kind of critique heterotopically, with an emphasis on other worlds and the relation of these to subjectivity and the unconscious.

After reading these six papers, written by research students and colleagues of the editor's, I thought about a context for my response: something to do with lines of filiation in both academic and psychoanalytical practice; and something to do with phenomenology. What came to mind was supervision, both psychoanalytical and academic. There is a sentence of Wittgenstein's that my psychoanalytical supervisor quotes and that I, in turn, use with supervisees, students, and, often, patients: 'All I know are the pictures painted in the stories you tell.' So, the first picture I reflected upon was to do with filiation, that is, influence and transference. Four of the six authors write about their research in a particular field of study. They call this 'empirical phenomenology'. Their influences, they say, are Giorgi (2002, 2006, 2009), Moustakas (1990), and Sela-Smith (2002). All I know are pictures. I could go to a university library and do some research, after which I could engage in a discussion of the quality of the representation of the field of study in these pictures, but, that would evade Wittgenstein's challenge.

There is always some anxiety about truth and authority – power-knowledge – in academic writing, interpretable, for example, in the way that one of the writers of the set of papers refers to Giorgi's approach as 'established'. Moustakas and Sela-Smith are represented in the pictures painted in the stories the researchers tell as posing a positive critique of Giorgi's approach and suggesting further procedures that the writers follow. These additional procedures formalise ways for the researchers to reflect on their implication in the objects and methods of their research and to produce what, following Merleau-Ponty, and as Julia Cayne, the author of 'Language as Gesture in Merleau-Ponty: Some implications for method in therapeutic practice and research' argues, we might call 'flesh'. The authors of 'Looking Like a Foreigner: foreignness, conformity and compliance in psychoanalysis', about racism, 'The private life of meaning – some implications for psychotherapy and psychotherapeutic research', about mental health nursing, 'Finding my voice: Telling stories with heuristic self-search inquiry', about schizophrenia, 'When working in a youth service, how do therapists experience humour with their clients?', about youth work, and 'What gets in the way of working with clients who have been sexually abused', about abuse, are most vivid when they talk about their own experience and most schematic and abstract when they talk about their research findings and procedure. It was only after reading the full set of papers that I got the picture; I got a sense of what they drew from Giorgi. And, my picture, painted in my stories, is a kind of deadpan punning: a Freudian-Lacanian way of letting the unconscious speak. The Lacanian style of interpretation I use here relies upon scansion.[1] That is, when commenting on these papers in a psychoanalytical style that echoes my teaching methods and, in turn, my work in the consulting room, I listen and I scan, and, as an interpretation, I stress *got; drew.*

When I use Wittgenstein's statement in a session with an analysand or supervisee, I'm pleased if they are deflected onto a question of fantasy, of what shapes and colours the pictures painted in their stories (Wittgenstein 2001, 1961/1974). Sometimes they say that their stories are shaped by a desire to please me or to challenge me. So, reading the set of papers psychoanalytically and in terms of the history of psychoanalysis, we're reminded that the field of study, is, in Madeleine and Willy Baranger's phrase, a transferential field (Baranger & Baranger 2015).[2] Traces of happenings in this transferential field are apparent, I argue, in researchers' writings, not just in the consulting room. Thus, I draw on Lacan and on Madeleine and Willy Baranger. All three were in dialogue with Merleau-Ponty, but, in institutional terms, they have different filiations.

So, to return to the papers in this journal, what's the field of study? What's an empirical phenomenology, insofar as a picture of this is painted in these writings? The picture painted in the stories told in the papers about the authors' empirical research (as in the last four papers) is a picture of research based on interviews with fellow practitioners or with people in therapy. My approach to research based on interviews is greatly influenced by Clifford Geertz's critique of oppositions between so-called 'native informants' and 'anthropological theorists' (Geertz 1973). Geertz's response to this dilemma was to use 'thick descriptions', rich descriptions in which 'theory' was immanent and which privileged the gestures and texture of the 'natives' speech. In his paper, Onel Brooks's insistence on himself as 'foreigner' is very much in that radical tradition. Rather than drawing on theory (for example, Ranjana Khanna on feminism, colonialism, and psychoanalysis or Emily Apter on language, postcolonialism, and national literatures), Brooks produces immanent critique from his subject position, arguing from the jarring address from a fellow passenger on a train, from conversations with colleagues, and from sessions with a patient, that his 'foreignness' gives him sure footing from which to argue his strongly and eloquently anti-racist position (Apter 2013; Khanna 2003).

I wonder, though, whether claiming that name and self-nominating as 'foreigner' might simply displace and re-iterate the colonial discourse of 'natives' and 'settlers' analysed so persuasively by Fanon (1963, 1967)? The author of Paper 1 responds to this irreducible dilemma by characterising modernism, including the hegemonic theories of modernity, as colonising and postmodernism as postcolonialist, but the theoretical claim is less nuanced than the phenomenological descriptions of the writer's encounters with strangers, colleagues, and patients. 'Foreigner' was Strachey's term, and it was very much of Strachey's time, as was the colonialist discourse of 'natives' that Brooks references. It might have been useful to have heard more about the differences in contemporary discourses of 'foreignness', although, as a genealogy of this term, the discussion of Strachey's usage makes a good case for the imbrication of psychoanalysis with the nexus of colonialism and psychoanalysis Brooks addresses.

Brooks mentions his unease with epistemological foundations. I share that scepticism, but I would argue that, rather than simply stopping at a scepticism about the foundations of knowledge, it is useful to argue, like

Levinas, that ethics, not epistemology, is the first philosophy (Levinas 1985). Ethics, the relation to the other, would help us make sense of the transformational possibilities found in listening and in recognition in our consulting rooms. The profound distress of a therapist mis-recognised on a train, as Brooks describes so vividly, or mis-recognised in conversation with colleagues and in their consulting room, can, after critical thought, lead to a practice based, as they argue, on an acknowledgement of their patient's specificity. Perhaps we might say 'difference', if it were not for Brooks's caution that in doing so, we would misidentify psychoanalysis as sameness, the problem that the author, by focusing on their "foreignness' articulates so clearly. Levinas's argument is not relationalist; his notion of our ethical relation as one that respects and is confounded by the radical alterity of the other is about witnessing, not recognition. But, as Jessica Benjamin argues of the philosophy that might underlie relationalist psychoanalysis, Honneth's notion of a non-Hegelian recognition is a philosophical grounding for our understanding of the moments of recognition in encounters in the consulting room (Benjamin 2017; Honneth 1996).

'Language as Gesture in Merleau-Ponty: Some implications for method in therapeutic practice and research', a thoughtful, sensitive exposition of Merleau-Ponty's writing, framed in terms of a relation to a psychoanalytical practice drawing upon Winnicott's notion of 'the spontaneous gesture', as discussed in the volume of Winnicott's letters, suggests that it is gesture and flesh that bring in what is left out in a reduction to essence. Julia Cayne presents Merleau-Ponty very well, showing how his work is relevant to psychoanalysts' practice. What I take away from Cayne, though, is a question: what does she mean by

> Reverie can be seen to be concerned with imagination and the poetic and as such resists positing being concerned with words that dream.

This strikes me as an interesting reversal. Reverie, to me, is dream-work: when the analyst dreams while awake and listening to the patient, this is a way past the analyst's resistance. But, to Cayne, reverie is resistance, twice. We scan the sentence in several ways. We scan and hear it as reverie resists the very notion of dream-work: 'reverie ... as such resists positing being concerned with words that dream'. Or, we scan and hear it as reverie is 'concerned with words that dream'; 'positing' is, for the writer, an unconscious process that reverie resists.

Read and re-read in the light of the unconscious as well as the authors' and research participants' intention, all six papers have flesh. In paper 1, the experience of racism in the present leads the author to call out racism in the history of psychoanalysis. Paper 2 embodies a pleasure in reading and explicating the philosophical text. Reading Paper 3 in terms of a sensitivity to flesh and gesture, what I hear is a tentativeness about saying, 'I', as in their discussion of 'Origins of the study',

> This study is rooted in two areas of experience personal to the main researcher. The first is linked to taking seriously one's experience. This is linked to how the main researcher had tried to transpose a former way of living as a Franciscan friar in a religious community onto working in mental health nursing

The enunciation is tentative; the statement uses the impersonal, 'one' and the third person, 'the main researcher'. The vocabulary of the statement places the enunciator in a transferential field and a history of academia in which status and authority are earned by nomination as 'main researcher'; McSherry *et al*. My association, as reader, is with my clinical work, and, in particular, with sessions in which the focus is on a patient's anxieties around gatekeeping and status in the academy. The disjunction between statement and enunciation is jarring, and so, McSherry, Loewenthal and Cayne's mention of 'abjection' in the subsequent paragraphs in not unexpected. But, abjection is just named: abjection is not a 'rich description' in Geertz's sense; abjection is not evoked, as it might be, for example, in a clinical session. I'm left wondering what is abject to McSherry et al. Is it what is shared with the interviewee, the shame at working on paperwork rather than on the therapeutic aspects of mental health nursing? Thus, 'being with another', the essence of what to the researcher is 'therapeutic' in mental health nursing, is therapeutic also to the researcher, personally. Their feeling of abjection resonates with the experiences of other researchers they've read and with the experience of other practitioners they study. The picture painted in the stories told by McSherry et al. is one of a sadness and regret that is both and neither the researcher's or the participants',

> *When she touched on how she came into nursing, her speech was full of pauses, stops and starts ... There was an intense sense of sadness ... There was an entangled grief here perhaps* [the researcher's and the participant's grief]. (Writer's italics and brackets, my ellipses)

As McSherry et al.'s parenthetic remark suggests, they are well aware of this. In this paper, the writers give a good sense of unconscious and conscious flows, key to both clinical and academic work.

From the stories they tell, the writers of the final four papers draw on a method, grounded in the work of a researcher, Giorgi, who, they explain, takes the idea of a phenomenological reduction and derives from it a process of reflection on the words of interviewees. In this process, the researcher can make 'essences'; they describe this as like the way a home-distiller can make hooch from whatever that stuff is in the cellar. If the unconscious comes into this process, it's the unconscious as cellar, tidied up in what, according to what the researchers say, are the sensible recommendations of Moustakas

(1990) and Sela-Smith (2002). It's a bit like a psychoanalytical supervision. If both the supervisor and the supervised are letting their unconscious have free range the session can be extraordinary or mundane, but, both possibilities are productive. There's a risk, but it's the risk of the question, 'are you talking about yourself or me?', which the 'native informant' vs 'anthropologist' opposition rules out. There's an anxiety about this, and so it's no wonder that Giorgi, Moustakas, and Sela-Smith, from the pictures painted by the writers of these papers, tend to go for specific practice recommendations. So many excellent academic researchers ask questions that are about themselves even more than they are about the objects of their research, that the self-reflective heuristics of Moustakas and Sela-Smith, as painted in the pictures of the authors of these final four papers, and then given free range, make for moving and lively discussion. But, it was only after having read all four of the papers about the authors' 'empirical phenomenological' studies that I began to understand that their research style – based, they say, on Giorgi – drew out what the researchers found to be common traits in the interviews and, they speculated, the interviewees. It was in the reflection on the authors' process (rather than interviewees' content) that I heard voice, that I sensed flesh. What the researchers called the 'essence', in the sketches of participants in their studies, seemed fleshless, abstract. The writers include a little of the grittiness of the participants' actual words or gestures, but, sometimes, even here, it is difficult to hear the unconscious speak. It seemed to me that what the researchers heard was what the participants intended to say, thoughtful and useful as it may be, but not unexpected.

But, in the present historical context, where 'research' so often means number-crunching, this focus on the meaningful intention of interviewees and researchers is important in itself. It is a pleasure to read four papers that give a sustained critique of their nuanced qualitative research, focusing on process as well as results. Because of the focus on critique, the authors of the papers are very clear that their research, rather than being budget-driven comparisons of the effectiveness of one or other response to human distress, is driven by an awareness of their own stakes as practitioners, researchers, and committed human beings. There's something existentialist in Sartre's sense: we choose. Or, in Merleau-Ponty's way of putting it, we are in and of the world (Merleau-Ponty 1968). So, as the papers in this special issue argue, if we are of the world, rather than standing a little above on a precariously objective platform, what does this mean for research?

Elizabeth Nicholl, as lead author of 'Finding my voice: Telling stories with heuristic self-search inquiry' presents a clear discussion of the influence on them of Moustakas and Sela-Smith. In addition to this self-reflectiveness about 'research', termed by them 'heuristic self-search enquiry', Nicholl gives a vivid sense of what I've been calling 'flesh'. Her focus is on a teenage diagnosis of schizophrenia which they overcame by self-silencing. The paper is thus a kind of coming-out. The reflection on voice and silence led them to conduct a research project on persons diagnosed with schizophrenia's experience of psychotherapy. Or, perhaps, as she says, her choice of a research topic for their PhD gave her the time and space to reflect on her own experience.

What I first carried away from my reading of her paper was a story that profoundly shocked me. She discloses a teenage diagnosis of psychosis to a psychotherapist who turns her away, refusing to accept her for therapy. My response as reader – my countertransference – is fury. This fury – my countertransference – is not addressed to the particular therapist, but, to the training institution. This institution would seem, I imagine, not to have availed themselves of the many opportunities for excellent training on working with psychosis. That is, I locate this object-relation, this *object little a*, in a neighbourhood bordering on the Imaginary region of my psyche, conceptualised as RSI, and experience myself there, in the Imaginary, as this emotion of fury.[3] Nicholl vividly describes her symptoms and her psychiatric treatment which, horrifyingly, included ECT and depo (injection under the skin of a long-term dose of medication). Depo deprives a person of agency, puts severe limits on any possibility of asserting control. Nicholl's remarkable and heart-warming story is of coming off the medication and finding her agency. However, she says, she silenced herself for many years, and when she began to self-disclose with the aim of analysing the effects of this early diagnosis in her therapy, she was met by what, to me, seems ignorance. That's the kindest word I can find for it.

Of course, what I know is only the picture painted in the stories you tell. In my countertransference, in a story I might tell in a supervision, I'm in a teaching room, talking about psychosis. I pay attention to my breathing, both as a way to contain the fury and as a way to project my voice so the class hears my words. The story has flesh; I'm thrown into my body, into my inhabited spaces, into my relationality with patients and students.[4]

I wonder, though, if the empirical phenomenology of the papers based on analysis of interviews with practitioners and patients, despite the researchers' intention, risks leading to a reduction to sameness, to identity-with-itself. Several of the researchers concluded by wondering whether their self-reflective musings on the research, while clarifying their thoughts and leading to some very interesting writing, left them with a question about investigator bias. They might hear what confirms their hypothesis more readily than they would hear what might disprove it; a problem that might be addressed by, for example, having another person do the coding. My question, though, is slightly different. If this particular empirical phenomenological method aims at what might be thought to be an underlying 'essence' (as Iana Trichova et al., says in their very useful discussion of what McSherry et al. calls the 'established' phenomenological method of Giorgi), how can what is 'counter, original, spare, strange' to the essence the study posits be written about (Hopkins 1953)?

Trichkova et al. and McSherry et al. explain what Talens was doing, in her paragraphs about the interviewees. These are intended as portraits of what the researcher considers, after a process of many-layered reflection or thought, to be a range of 'essences' underlying what she heard in the interviewees' words. But, it's a bit like the tortoise and the hare; that illustration of never arriving. Each step in the 'method' requires another self-reflective step; each successive step also falls short of a receding horizon of meaning. So, Talens describes 7 ways of using and relating to humour in the consulting room, schematising one per interviewee. The interviewees and researcher emphasise the varying uses of humour as communication and expression. The participants worked with young persons, and they speak about how humour was used by young persons who might have been referred by authority, rather than choosing therapy. There is a little of the flesh, the words of the interviewees. There is scope for taking this further, perhaps by discussion of Freud's joke book; the joke about the persons travelling to Lemburg or Krakow turns on Lemburg (Lvov, Lviv) as on the Russian side of the Pale, a border one might not be able to cross under one's own name; a joke that takes a blow at empire so indirect as to be difficult to hear.[5]

So, if it is essence they are aiming at, rather than flesh, the paper clearly identifies and sketches a typology for the different uses of humour they've found in the work with young people. However, more 'rich description' of the voices and gestures of young persons in therapy and analysts, engaged in clinical dialogue, would be needed for the argument to be taken further.

'What gets in the way of working with clients who have been sexually abused', as I've indicated, gives a reader the clearest sense of the 'method' introduced by Giorgi and the innovations of the next persons in the line of filiation, Moustakas and Sela-Smith. Like the paper on racism and the paper on a teenage diagnosis of schizophrenia, this author gives us much of the flesh called for in Julia Cayne's on Merleau-Ponty. Trichkova, in a discussion of working with patients who have been sexually abused, has interviewed a number of fellow practitioners – more than 5, less than 10, as in the other qualitative papers in this group – and found that they have common concerns with countertransference. The participants and researcher focus on countertransference as baggage we ought to leave outside the consulting room. That is Freud's sense, rather than, for example, Searles' or the relationalists' sense, which would be, in contrast, to take countertransference as a source of information about what the patient finds it difficult to think, difficult to process (Searles 1979; Searles 1986; Benjamin 2017). In Trichkova's phrase, countertransference is 'what gets in the way' of the work. Typing that, a question of scansion comes up: 'the way of the work' is the route; 'in the way' is the baggage we leave downstairs by the coats. The researcher writes a letter to a patient who left after a single session and posts the letter here, in their writing. The researcher is finding her voice in writing rather than in speech. The patient, she considers, projected a stultifying silence, with which the practitioner identified. The parallel process, the enactment, is still to be brought into speech, still to be analysed.[6] But, in the unsent letter, the practitioner finds her voice. The silence, the parallel process, is now a space for thought.

To conclude, I'd like to return to my remark about witnessing and recognition. Lacan argued that the dynamic Hegel analysed as master/slave is a way of theorising masochism, which Lacan considered to be basic to the human condition. As Laplanche later argued, every baby is vulnerable to the intrusions of their primary care giver (Laplanche 2016). The infant, becoming a speaking being, tries to give meaning to these intrusions: the enigmatic signifier, which, first of all, is a question, 'who does the mother love?' The risk we take when interpreting is that patients might find an interpretation intrusive, as if we are telling them what and how to think. In response to this, Lacanians try to keep their interpretations enigmatic, so that patients do the thinking. Relationalists draw on their countertransference in coming up with interpretations and often try to discuss the interpretations in a more dialogic way.

Patients sometimes ask questions about psychoanalytical theory: usually, I'll just say 'hmmm' or ask them what the question means to them. But, recently, and more than once, I've responded directly to a question or comment about psychoanalytical theory, thinking that my patient might be talking about different ways to conceptualise what they were experiencing. These patients are lovers of reading; intellectuals. Their demand was that I recognise this. If, in response to their demand, I show something of my own pleasure in reading, I risk imposing my own fantasy on them. But, if we can find the right way to dialogue about this, in doing so, we'll move onto that uncertain terrain where we might construct alternatives to power-knowledge, ways of thinking other than master/slave. In each of these recent cases, the patient said, 'oh' or 'thanks' and changed the subject. It could be that they'd demanded from me what they thought might win my love and realised in getting it that it wasn't what they wanted. But, their silence could also have indicated that they were sublimating, making something of the theory.

Do we take the gamble that patients are sublimating, binding drives (and thus reducing anxiety) in a way that involves what Lacan called the symbolic? When I was in graduate school, we read translations of the French feminists, who argued that we could write ourselves into a new symbolic and a new imaginary. In a more modest but perhaps more achievable way, that happens in speech. However, the subjectivity and world in and of the consulting room is neither new nor old. The history of psychoanalysis is not progress towards utopia (or dystopia).

When enacting a dialogue – in our consulting rooms, in seminars, or over coffee or wine – sometimes we construct *heterotopias*, times, places, and *communities* of patients and analysts in which, despite and through our intention to construct other spaces, the dynamics of the world in which we are thrown are played out (Foucault 1984). Community is my fantasy, my illusion. Perhaps I'm imposing on my patients in sometimes using my countertransference, rather than always witnessing, always respecting the radical otherness of patients. But, I think it's vital. The racism Brooks calls out or the fear of madness written about by Nicholl are not extra-analytical concerns that destroy our psychoanalytical utopia. Heterotopic other spaces are traversed by lines of force, that is, by racism, fear of madness, and also more positive political forces, but these forces are not only impersonal; they are not only abstract. One way of thinking of the relation of subjectivity to these worlds of ours is Merleau-Ponty's notion that we are in and of the world. Another is Badiou's idea of worlding (Badiou 2013). It's easier to see that heterotopias are worlded by those who live in them, but, I'd say this is true of all worlding, even the most mundane. It's strange, it's estranging, to think of psychoanalytical practice as part of worlding, but perhaps that enlivens it.

I became familiar with the notion of heterotopia as a teenage science fiction fan, in the 1970s, at a time when feminist and queer writers and readers were raising questions about imagined worlds. We'd moved to the UK from the US and we stayed here year by year rather than making an explicit decision to consider ourselves immigrants. I was primed to think of alienation by thinking about aliens and humans in imagined worlds. But, my focus was deflected from alienation to thinking about the worlds imagined in the writings and now in my patients' words. Their projects – and mine – sometimes make bubbles, time and space for our ways of living and meaning-making. In my experience, these communities tend to break up. They don't last more than a few decades and so we are reduced to thinking of our words as less fragile and temporary than our deeds. This is plainly not the case and so it is *heterotopic*. Recognition, I think, happens most easily when there's an overlap in worldings. When this happens, social bonds are forged, making the heterotopia briefly real. This can overwhelm, and we fall back into the masochism that seduces us, making our heterotopias ever smaller and more beleaguered but, still, they exist, they flourish.

Let me give an example of the overlapping communities of which analysts are part. For reasons of confidentiality, I'll focus on people linked by writing and reading, a bit like what happens in science fiction fandom. In the 1970s, that is, at the time when I was, as a science fiction reader, thinking about heterotopia, I applied to university. My mother offered me the possibility of starting to build up a portfolio to accompany my university application, handing me two books she'd been asked to review, one of which was a collection of essays by analysts at the Women's Therapy Centre. I remember I liked one of the essays very much and said so in the review. Many years later, I met that analyst, Vivien Burgoyne, and her husband, Bernard, both of whom are people of whom, now, I'm very fond and whom I admire greatly. Now, we're part of the same psychoanalytical community, but doesn't it make sense to argue that our history – as in and of the world – goes back to these brief connections, in writing, in the 1970s? It is in the world that our histories and communities overlap, so it is 'intentionality' in the phenomenological sense – relation to the world rather than 'intentionality' in the conscious, ends-rational sense – that brings about change.

Notes

1. Whatever the orientation, psychoanalysis is based on listening. In a Lacanian style, you'd listen for rhythm and tone in your patient's words and voice, just as you'd scan a poem or prose for structure and rhythm. When I echo a key word in the patient's discourse I often do so in a different tone or rhythm. If they hear that as an interpretation a dialogue would open up; or maybe we'd cut – we'd stop at that moment, either for ten minutes or until the next session.
2. Following Madeleine and Willy Baranger, I use the term transferential field. Both the analyst and the analysand bring something that repeats to what's happening in the consulting room. What we each bring interacts, as if we are two centres of gravity in a gravity field. See the Barangers' discussion of transference and countertransference in 'The Analytical Situation as a Dynamic Field' in Nydia Lisman-Pieczanski and Alberto Pieczanski (2015).
3. In the late Seminars, Lacan argues that there is a third topology for the psyche. The first topology is Freud's Unconscious; Preconscious; Conscious. The second topology is Freud's Ego; Superego; Id. The third is Lacan's Real; Symbolic; Imaginary. The London tube map is topological, it shows you how to get there from here. But, when you get out of the station you might find yourself confused. The relations don't translate directly onto a street map. So, these topologies are about relations through which subjectivation and objectalisation cohere or deliquesce. Or, in terms of Freud's second drive theory, there is binding and unbinding. My interpretation and use of Lacan's third topology is based on my reading of Freud's papers 'On Narcissism' and 'The Splitting of the Ego in the Process of Defence.' Although there are so-called 'pathological' fixations and thus developments of narcissism grounded in an attempt at self-cure, as a process, narcissism is key to the development of normal/neurotic structures. Lacan indicates these normal/neurotic narcissisms and splittings by using a bar / to write a barred or split subject and object. The point is that normal/neurotic subjectivation and objectalisation involve differentiation within and between subject and object. In another perspective, this is to do with being able to bear absence, i.e. as Andre Green argues in *The Work of the Negative*, (Green, 2002, 2006, 2009), to do with the work of negation. In the late seminars, building on his sympathetic critique of Balint in the early seminars, Lacan separates the object relation into three processes, the unbarred Other, the barred Other, and the object little a. The 'crocodile mother' would be an unbarred Other. A barred Other would be split and humanised as effect of the work of negation. The object little a is the object cause of desire, whoever that might be for you.
4. I'd like to thank Haya Oakley for her theory and practice, a respectful and profoundly caring way to work with and supervise work with severe psychosis. Essential texts are Lacan (1966). 'On a Question Prior to Any Possible Treatment of Psychosis' and Roustang, 1976/1982). 'Toward a Theory of Psychosis'. I teach Lacan and Roustang and recommend them to supervisees

in order to transmit this way of working with psychosis. Roustang argues that what I've been calling the 'transferential field' is a stage, a theatre, in the work with people with psychosis. He argues that they, our psychotic patients, put us, the analysts, on the stage, and they are the theatre, not the director or the playwright. Further theorists, those who, I would argue, theorise ways of including 'experience-near' material in teaching and writing, are also central to my teaching and writing. Thus, for example, in this paper, I draw on field theory. But, although I argue that an attunement to the transferential field is often a source of interpretations, I do not interpret when working in the consulting room with severe psychosis. Instead, I bring material from the transferential field to supervision (given and received), teaching, and writing. Those discussions – our consideration of affects and concepts – inform my work in the consulting room. This helps me experience – rather than evade – the anguish in this work and thus to continue with it. By the way, one patient with whom, as I mention above, I briefly discussed theory in a session was psychotic and one was neurotic; a difference that made no difference.
5. 'Two Jews meet in a railway carriage at a station in Galicia. "Where are you going?" asks one. "To Cracow" was the answer. "What a liar you are!" broke out the other. "If you say you are going to Cracow, you want me to believe you are going to Lemberg. But I know you are going to Cracow. So why are you lying to me?"' *Jokes and their Relation to the Unconscious*, Sigmund S. Freud (1905) S.E. 8 p. 115. The humour plays on the logic of truth and lies. The cultural meanings are linked to this play on truth, lies, and logic. Lemburg was beyond the Pale, that is, within the Russian empire. A Jewish man of military age, subject to Russian conscription, might well have used forged papers to continue his journey to Krakow. Krakow was a centre of Hassidic scholarship.
6. What isn't processed returns. In particular, if what repeats isn't processed in the psyche (through dreams and slips of the tongue, etc.), it returns in the body or in enactment. Enactments used to be called acting out, but that's very judgemental, and so, nowadays, we call them enactments.

Disclosure statement

No potential conflict of interest was reported by the authors.

References

Apter, E. (2013). *Against world literature: On the politics of untranslatability*. Verso.
Badiou, A. (2013). *Logics of worlds*. translated by Alberto Toscano. Bloomsbury.
Baranger, M., & Baranger, W. (2015). The analytical situation as a dynamic field" in Nydia Lisman-Pieczanski and Alberto Pieczanski. In *The pioneers of psychoanalysis in South America*. Routledge.

Benjamin, J. (2017). *Beyond doer and done to.* Routledge Taylor and Francis.
Fanon, F. (1963). *The wretched of the earth.* translated by C. Farringdon. Grove Press.
Fanon, F. (1967). *Black skin white masks.* translated by C.L. Markmann. Grove Press.
Foucault, M. (1984). *Of other spaces: Utopias and heterotopias.* translated by Jay Miscowiec. Architecture/Mouvement/Continuité.
Freud, S. (1905). S.E. 8. *Jokes and their relation to the unconscious.*
Freud, S. (1957). *On narcissism.* S.E. XIV. London: Hogarth Press, 1966.
Freud, S. (1964). *The splitting of the ego in the process of defence.* S.E. XXII. London: Hogarth Press, 1966
Geertz, C. (1973). *The interpretation of cultures.* Basic Books.
Giorgi, A. (2002, 2006, 2009). *The descriptive phenomenological method in psychology: a modified husserlian approach.* Pittsburgh, PA: Duquesne University Press.
Honneth, A. (1996). *The Struggle For Recognition.* translated by Joel Anderson. MIT Press.
Hopkins, G. M. (1953). *Poems and prose.* Oxford UP.
Khanna, R. (2003). *Dark continents: Psychoanalysis and colonialism.* Duke UP.
Lacan, J., & Lacan, J. (1966). On a question prior to any possible treatment of psychosis. In B. Fink (Ed.), *Écrits.* Norton.
Lacan, J. (1977). *Seminar XI, the four fundamental concepts of psychoanalysis.* translated by Alan Sheridan. Norton.
Laplanche, J. (2016). *New foundations for psychoanalysis.* translated by Jonathan House. The Unconscious in Translation.
Levinas, E. (1985). *Ethics and Infinity, Conversations with Philippe Nemo.* translated by Richard Cohen. Duquesne UP.
Merleau-Ponty, M. (1968). *The visible and the invisible.* translated by Alphonso Lingis. Northwestern UP.
Moustakas, C. E. (1990). *Heuristic research : design, methodology, and applications.* Sage Publications, Inc. doi:10.4135/9781412995641
Roustang, F. (1976/1982). Toward a theory of psychosis. In N. Lukacher (Ed.), *Dire mastery* (pp. 132–156). American Psychiatric Press.
Searles, H. (1979). *Countertransference.* International UP.
Searles, H. (1986). *My work with borderline patients.* Jason Aronson Inc.
Sela-Smith, S. (2002). Heuristic research: A review and critique of moustakas's method. *Journal of Humanistic Psychology, 42*(3), 53–88. doi:10.1177/0022167802423004
Wittgenstein, L. (1961/1974). *Tractatus logico-philosophicus.* translated by D.F. Pears and B.F. McGuiness. Routledge Taylor and Francis.
Wittgenstein, L. (2001). *Philosophical investigations* (translated by G.E.M. Anscombe. P.M.S. Hacker and Joachim Schulte. (1953. 2nd Edn 1958. 3rd Edition). Wiley-Blackwell.

Reflections on the tensions between openness and method in experientially oriented research and psychotherapy

Steen Halling

ABSTRACT
In this article, as a phenomenological psychologist, researcher, and professor I offer reflections on the six articles that make up this special edition of the Journal. I respond to each in some detail, addressing issues around the challenges of using phenomenological methods, understanding them adequately, and the challenge of finding ways of studying phenomena systematically while also remaining retaining an attitude of humility about our capacity to arrive at understandings that do justice to the accounts of research participants.

I have found that the most productive dialogues take place when there is a mixture of agreement and disagreement allowing for a clarification of one's own understanding and point of view as one takes into account and struggles with perspectives that that one had not previously encountered. This has very much been the case for me in this instance.

I am very pleased to have the opportunity to contribute to this special edition of EJPC, organized by Dr. Loewenthal, on Critical Existential-Analytic Psychotherapies. The issues that his introduction and the articles that follow raise are of great importance to the community of psychotherapists who do in-depth therapy, whether they explicitly identify as working within an existential, phenomenological or analytic tradition. My colleague Enrico Gnaulati has recently published a book where he raises some of the same concerns that are expressed in the contributions to this special edition. In *Saving Talk Therapy: How Health Insurers, Big Pharma, and Slanted Science are Ruining Good Mental Health Care* (Gnaulati, 2018), he provided a compelling and spirited argument for the value of psychotherapy for individuals and for society. Drawing upon a wide range of research, he also does the public and the mental health profession a great service by questioning the often extravagant claims made for the effectiveness and safety of psychiatric medication, and the overstated benefits of quick-fix therapies. As someone who is involved in the education of master level psychotherapists, I also noted that Gnaulati raised an alarm about how Cognitive Behavioral Therapy's favored status in graduate programs prevents trainee therapists from acquiring the relationship skills necessary to caringly and carefully treat patients. There are many other voices that in harmony with those of Gnaulati and Loewenthal are speaking up for experientially focused approaches to psychotherapy as well as to research. These voices remind us that 'evidence' based practice is not going to take over the world of mental health. In what follows I will refer to some of these sources as I discuss the articles in this special edition of EJPC.

One of the key principles of phenomenology is that all knowledge is perspectival. We are historically, culturally, and linguistically situated embodied beings. Accordingly, I will briefly describe my own perspective. I am a phenomenological psychologist (in the United States) who teaches, practices psychotherapy, and conducts qualitative research. With regard to psychotherapy I am one of a small group of graduate students and faculty who started a non-profit counseling service for low income people twenty years ago. This enterprise grew out of our concern that the mental health system did not serve poor people who needed and wanted longer term psychotherapy (Halling et al., 2006a).

As a researcher and teacher, I am quite familiar with widely practiced qualitative research methods such Interpretative Phenomenological Analysis, Heuristic Inquiry, and the Descriptive Phenomenological Approach. My own research experience has been working with small groups carrying out phenomenological studies using, an approach that is process oriented and based on specific principles that provide structure and direction. For example, the collaborative group analysis requires sustained focus on descriptions of the specific phenomenon from research participants as well as the researchers (Halling et al., 2006b). My basic viewpoint is 'ecumenical' in the sense that I appreciate the contributions that various approaches offer (Halling, 2014). Genuine appreciation includes having a keen eye for the limitations as well as the strengths of specific studies and theories.

As I read the articles included in this volume, I felt like someone who has stepped into an art exhibit with multiple paintings. Even though the artists have a shared orientation, their paintings are also distinctive. Some are complex and puzzling, others are readily accessible, and still others raised questions to which I had not previously given much attention. In what follows I will comment selectively on each contribution, discussing overall themes that I am particularly interested in or that I think are of special significance.

I begin with the article with Yana Trichkova as the lead author on 'What gets in the way of working with clients who have been sexually abused.' The issue is of obvious importance and the approach of the research is relatively straightforward. Following the Heuristic Inquiry approach (based on Moustakas's work) makes perfect sense given that the motivation for this study came from a particularly disturbing psychotherapy session. This woman described her sexual abuse graphically but with flat affect and then not return for her next appointment. This incident gave rise to the researcher's exploration of her own sexual abuse as she tried to understand if there was something about her own response to the client that led her not to return. Subsequently, after an extensive self-examination, she recruited eight therapists and interviewed them about their experiences about sexually abused clients. The findings are presented in the form of a listing of themes such such as mistakenly pressuring the client to talk about disturbing issues and guilt, in the case of a male therapist, in the face of clients who had been abused by men. Most of the findings coincided with the issues presented in the existing literature except for vicarious traumatization which did not come up with these therapists. The authors emphasize that the preparation for working with abuse clients must include a working through of personal traumas and conflicts about gender and sexuality. This is an important point, an almost commonsensical one, but apparently it has been neglected in practice. A related and equally important point is that therapists need to learn to tolerate their own emotional responses to what they hear, be it rage at the perpetrator or a drive to 'rescue' the client. The original study included individual depictions of the interviewees as well as composite depictions but these were omitted from the articles, presumably because of length limitations. These depictions, along with specific quotes presented in the context of a particular therapy relationship, would have helped to make the discussion more vivid and helpful as did the initial description of the session with the client who left such a deep impression on the author. In their 1999 article setting forth criteria for evaluating qualitative research, Elliott, Fischer, and Rennie recommend that author ground their presentation in examples and create resonance with readers. This study does both through the one detailed account but the rather generalized consideration of the contribution of the eight research participants makes it harder for the reader to step into their shoes. Perhaps one of the risks of the Heuristic Inquiry Method is that it predisposes researchers to give primary emphasis to their own experience.

The second article that employed a heuristic approach, entitled "Finding my voice: Telling stories with heuristic self-search inquiry, also deals with the personal experiences of therapists, specifically those who have been given a diagnosis of schizophrenia. The lead author, Elizabeth Nicholl, was given a diagnosis of schizophrenia as a young adult but recovered more despite than because of the psychiatric treatment she received. Her recovery was largely due to her own initiative and support of friends and family while the psychiatric treatment she received was largely unhelpful. Subsequently, she hid her psychiatric experience for years. Not until she became a doctoral student in psychotherapy did she consider revisiting that experience and the shame that surrounded it; in fact, it became the focus of her doctoral dissertation. In this article Elizabeth Nicholl highlights her own circumstances and personal development.

Those of us in the mental health community who fall more or less into the depressive and anxiety disorder spectrums (as Freud said, all of us are more or less neurotic) are indebted to the first-hand accounts of healers who have written about their own experience of psychosis and have thus given us a glimpse into a world of experiences that otherwise we could only speculate about. There is a long tradition of such accounts, such as Anton Boisen's (1960) account, *Out of the Depths*, and more recently Patrick Howell's (2000) *Reducing the Storm to a Whisper*. Boisen worked as a hospital chaplain and was himself hospitalized several times. Fr. Howell was a Jesuit priest who drew upon his experience of psychosis in his work with parishioners and students. Finally, the book *Exploring identities of psychiatric survivor therapists: Beyond us and them* (Adame et al., 2017) addresses the experiences of psychiatric survivors who are also mental therapists and activists engaging in the struggle to create more humane approaches to treatment.

The current article is also concerned with addressing problems with the psychiatric treatment approaches generally available. It is distinctive in that the lead author takes us through her intensive and year long struggle to confront her experience of shame and resistance using Sela-Smith's Heuristic Self-Inquiry. This is a modification of Moustakas' method in which Sela-Smith's prioritizes an immersion in self-exploration and fully expressing this experience rather than aligning it with the accounts of co-researchers and thus risking diminishing its distinctive nature. It is not self-evident to me why such an alignment would occur if one takes a phenomenological approach that recognizes that there may be significant variations in multiple accounts of the same phenomenon. But that is another issue.

The article by Onel Brooks 'Looking like a foreigner: Foreignness, conformity and compliance in psychoanalysis' is an excellent discussion of the problematic side of psychoanalysis, namely, its failure to fully take into account class, race, and culture. The author, a practicing analytic psychotherapist and a visible minority male, suggests that there are two ways in which one can take up the discipline: as 'a human technology, universally applicable to all people at all times in all places, or on the other hand, a cultural practice with the means for opening up conversations about how we experience and relate in and beyond the consulting room.' One of the most striking examples of the latter is Peter Lawner (1981) who addressed the challenge of facing the unknown in psychotherapy. Lawner wrote, 'As therapists we often move in darkness in which nothing can be seen' (p. 306). This attitude stands in contrast to what the author describes as characteristic of much of psychoanalysis, even today. Based on his own experience and a review of related literature, he argues that many psychoanalysts still adhere to the notion that their discipline is a science of the mind that can be applied universally. Doing so, he protests, does violence to the persons being treated because the treatment based on this assumption of universal applicability imposes concepts and interpretations on the patient without regard to his or her background and circumstances. Further, Onel Brooks describes how he has frequently run into colleagues whose training had been in traditional psychoanalysis and who questioned whether he was truly an analyst since his training was from a more 'liberal' institute. One of the powerful features of this article is a case presentation of the author's s work with a patient who had a working-class background and had run into stereotyping from his fellow students and others in his social circle who came from privileged backgrounds. This case presentation demonstrates the power of an open-ended and exploratory approach to psychoanalysis. Although the author does not use the term, I think his approach could aptly be described as a phenomenological version of psychoanalysis.

Humour plays an important role in the field of mental health. In a just published book, Max Heinrich (2020) writes of his work as a clinical psychologist in inpatient settings in the United States. In his introduction, he writes, humor 'has been a necessary shield as I continued my work in increasingly rigid and dehumanizing institutions' (Heinrich, 2020, p. 1.) I think anyone who has worked in the mental health field will readily identify with this sentiment. Hence I read the study (lead author Patricia Talens) on how therapists working with youth experienced humour with their clients with much interest. As the authors point out Freud and others have discussed how the use of humour can be risky insofar as it often has hidden meanings and dimensions that are counter to the purpose of therapeutic interventions, including hostility and concealment of anxious feelings. As they also point out, studies of the experience of therapists with humour are hard to find.

Their method of analyzing the transcripts from interviews with seven practitioners is an odd variation of Giorgi's (2009) Descriptive Phenomenological Method (DPM) to analyze the transcripts from interviews with seven practitioners. Unfortunately, no demographic data is provided, making it harder to make sense some of their findings. For example, they state that 'feelings of intimacy and unity were expressed non-verbally, providing a release of sexual tension.' Without discussing the contexts or providing quotes, I was unsure as to who was attracted to whom and who experienced tension or even the age of the therapists or the clients. More generally in presenting their findings, the researchers wrote up a portrait of each interviewee's responses under the heading of a distinctive theme such as humour holds power, humour connects, and humour is an emotion.

This presentation is confusing because it creates the impression that each research participant's account is different from the rest. There is an additional problem in that the 'essence' (or synthesis) that the researchers arrived at does not look like an essential structure but more like a definition of humour, such as the statement that humour is a form of communication. Moreover, the initial overview of Giorgi's method is incomplete; steps 3 through 5 are collapsed into one step. Finally, their critique of Giorgi's method does not make much sense. He fails, they argue, to explain what is meant by disciplinary languages. They should have referred to Giorgi's 2009 book where he states that 'each meaning unit, originally expressed in the participant's own words, is transformed by the researchers by means of a careful descriptive process into psychological pertinent expressions without using the jargon of mainstream psychology' (p. 137). This statement, it seems to me, gives the researcher a lot of latitude as to what kind of language to use. In addition, once one has arrived at a basic structure for the phenomenon, one can use that as a point of departure for elaboration and discussion (for an example of this, see Toback et al.'s, 2018 study of envy among executives). To be clear, I am not arguing that the Giorgi method is without limitations but I am suggesting that the criticisms raised by these researchers are less than convincing.

The article that I tackled next is one of the most complex in this selection. 'Language as gesture in Merleau-Ponty: Some implications for method in therapeutic practice and research' looks at the creative use of language. The author, Julia Cayne, refers to the phrase 'through a glass darkly' as an example of the creative use of language. Unfortunately, she wrongly attributes this phrase to Shakespeare rather than to St. Paul (1 Corinthians, Ch 13. v12). But from there, it is uphill! The scope and depth of the author's argument is, as I said, complex, and includes discussion of Winnicott, Saussure, Stern, Merleau-Ponty, and Bachelard, and concludes with a critique of phenomenology as leaning (my wording) toward positivism. Simply put, the author advocates for a recognition of language as fluid and dynamic as well as constituting a system in which we participate. Here she aligns herself with Merleau-Ponty (1962) who distinguishes between *la parole* referring to speech as creative expression which is an embodied and creative expression of genuine thoughts and feelings in response to the concrete situation in which one is engaged, and 'la langue'. The latter is language as a prexisting system in which we participate and which shapes our lives.

Since I have made a similar argument about the use of language (Halling, 2002) I will refer briefly to it here and then raise two points with regard to this article. In her book, *Amazing Grace*, Kathleen Norris

(1998) points to the static and sometimes even dead quality of everyday speech. Like the author of this article, she was impressed by the creative nature of the spontaneous speech of children. In a pedagogical experiment of sorts, she asked her elementary school children to sit still, and then to write about what this was like for them. When they wrote about this experience, which was a novel one for most of them, they were remarkably creative. For example, one little girl wrote 'Silence reminds me to take my soul with me wherever I go' (Norris, 1998, p. 17). In following up on this quote and others like it, I wrote:

> Approaching experiences from a new perspective, seeing them "as if for the first time," leads us to poetic and innovative use of language. This may be a risky path to take but it is a risk that can be avoided only at considerable cost. We risk sounding overly "subjective, or "unscientific," but the alternative is that we rely too much on lifeless abstraction and the clichés of our disciplines. (Halling, 2002, p. 30).

The above is basically in agreement with the position taken by this author, if I am understanding her correctly. My first concluding comment is that authentic speech does not have to be original or creative precisely since speech is embodied expression. I am not suggesting that this statement is at odds with the thesis of this article but I think it is important to keep it in mind. A simple example will serve to illustrate this point. Years ago, I worked in a hospital where one of the patients who had a diagnosis of catatonic schizophrenia did a lot of work around the ward. He hardly ever spoke but one day he walked up to the hospital superintendent and said, 'I want to be paid for my work.' We were startled at this clear expression of personal desire which would have been commonplace coming from anyone else.

Second, I am not convinced that using a method, be it IPA or Giorgi's method, necessarily or even typically, leads to 'deadness" or pushes us toward positivism. I am basing this assertion on my experience as a teacher and a researcher. The most obvious point is that methods are taken up differently by different researchers whether this is encouraged. As we know Jonathan Smith et al. (2009) explicitly allows or encourages modifications in his approach to analysis where it is indicated according to the judgment of the researcher. Giorgi (2009) presents his method as fixed regarding the steps involved but as I have learned from reading studies using his method this does not change the fact that the method is embodied differently by different people. To use quick and undoubtedly inadequate comparison, some researchers approach *methods* the way Fundamentalists approach the Bible and others more as do Liberal Christians. Most importantly, I have noticed that as my students go through steps outlined by Giorgi or J. Smith steps they look at the description they are working with in a new way and seeing it more 'as if for the first time' (Halling, 2014). There is a difference, I would argue, between using a method and being controlled by it. And, as this example shows, methods can break us out of our habitual patterns of thinking and perceiving.

I do not believe we can escape enacting some versions of method whether in our daily lives or in our professional practice. As a case in point, one of my colleagues with whom I co-taught an undergraduate course noted that I had a characteristic way of responding to certain kinds of questions from students. My response, he commented, turned the question into an opportunity for dialogue rather than simply ending the interaction with an answer. Was this consistent pattern a method, even though I was not explicitly aware of it? The word 'method' has multiple meanings and I would argue the above example falls within the definition of method as a systematic approach to a problem or challenge. On the other hand, methods are sometimes equated with techniques. Techniques, according to William Barrett, are neither flexible nor responsive. In his book *The Illusion of Technique*, Barrett (1979) argues that faith in techniques as solutions in human affairs is an illusion because they are mistakenly thought to work regardless of context, can be taught to anyone because they consist of discrete steps, and do not involve interpretation or discernment in their application. So while I agree that method as technique does close off exploration in research, method, in the broader sense, may well work to deepen our understanding and the range of questions we ask.

The article entitled 'The private life of meaning – some implications for psychotherapy and psychotherapeutic research', with Anthony McSherry as lead author, presents issues similar to the ones I have discussed above. It describes a fascinating study on the nature of therapeutic interactions in the lives of ten nurses. First, the topic was explored through Giorgi's method. Then the authors proposed a second and more fluid approach based on selected writings of Husserl, Merleau-Ponty and Heidegger. McSherry refers to his experience of moving from being a Franciscan Friar (an order dedicated to missionary work and service) to taking up the vocation of being a mental health work. This transition, as far as I can tell (his account is rather enigmatic), involved a challenging adjustment to a new way of being of service. The conclusion he drew from this experience is that one must pay close attention to the context in which behavior is embedded in order to adequately understand it. In this new context he recognized that some of the nurses interacted with patients in a way that was therapeutic, and that this involved stepping beyond standard procedural approaches to relating in a more personal way to those who were in distress.

I have no issue with the general argument that the Giorgi method has specific limitations and is not the best approach to tackle certain questions and phenomena. However, McSherry's description of his use of Giorgi's method is incomplete so it is difficult to evaluate to what extent the problems that arose came from the method itself or how it was taken up or both. For example, it is not clear what the interview question was or how the interviews were conducted. As I read the brief sections of transcript included it seemed as if the participants were asked about their understanding of the therapeutic rather than focusing specifically on an experience that they regarded as therapeutic. If this is true it is at odds with the DPM emphasis on focusing on concrete experiences. Did the researchers as part of their analysis come up with individual structures which could have included richer presentations of the nuances and complexity of the transcripts unlike the more abstract and condensed general structure? Perhaps McSherry et al thought that these aspects of their research were not especially relevant given that their primary aim was to demonstrate the limitations of the DPM and the necessity of a more open-ended fluid approach to phenomenology?

I am not, for the most part, a practitioner of the Giorgi method. However, having read great many studies and dissertations using the DPM approach, I would certainly concur that at least a fair number of them included a general structure that was removed from lived experience. This does not by itself mean that the studies and findings were not valuable and insightful but they did not emphasize the more sensual and personal aspects of the interviewees' experience. However, there are several ways that one can bring to the foreground the richness of the interviewees' stories, whatever method one uses. One is the effective use of quotes and the second is to provide in-depth summaries of the individuals' situations and accounts. Thirdly, as in the case of the Toback et al. (2018) study of envy, mentioned above, one can take the general structure as a point of departure for a detailed and focused discussion of various aspects of the constituents of the participants accounts. In any case, there are approaches to phenomenological analysis that are aligned with the authors' perspective as they outline it at the end of their article. Van Manen's (1997) approach to researching lived experience is one example and many nursing researchers have followed his principles. He too is opposed to coding or analyzing phenomenological data in a systematic manner (Van Manen, 2017). The approach that my colleagues and I have been using for the over three decades has at its core dialogue among the researchers and dialogue with the phenomenon (Halling et al., 2006b). As I have stated, above it involves following basic principles (e.g., focus on the phenomenon and developing trust among the researchers) and goes through basic stages in the research process but does not follow prescribed steps. Part of the strength of the method is that the dialogue among the researchers fosters richer and more experience-near articulation of the findings. As we describe the dialogue with the phenomenon we explicitly acknowledge that we participate in what we study, that it is not something 'out there' with which we have an 'objective' relationship.

I end my reflections and commentaries on this article with reflections on the careful and thought-provoking synthesis of phenomenological philosophers that the authors provide. Many of these points are ones with which I agree and that also ones that come up either implicitly or explicitly in the other five articles. Further, they seem to be at the core of what this special edition has as its underlying vision. My rephrasing of these points and the way I qualify them may be at odds, in some cases, with what the writers intended. But as many of them emphasize, one's understanding of the other is always tentative and incomplete.

Part of the psychotherapy process and the research process involves moving into the unknown, as Lawner (1981) points out and one's findings are always tentative, open to revision and further elaboration. In her book on phenomenological assessment, Constance Fischer (1994) emphasizes the importance of using the past tense in one's reports as a reminder that the person assessed is always in motion, as are all of us. As the authors themselves say, 'Something could change if she (the nurse who was interviewed again, perhaps the whole landscape' (p. –). They also emphasize that there is an ever-present risk of getting caught up in method, theory, ideas or a particular language. This is an important consideration but by itself it is misleading. As Gadamer (1988) stated, we are necessarily rooted kin a tradition and proceed from a preunderstanding, In fact, we necessarily proceed from a preunderstanding and that is not inherently a problem insofar as we enter into an ongoing and open ended exploration of the topic at hand. Similarly, Merleau-Ponty (1964), in his chapter on The Philosopher and Sociology, asserts that:

> The point is that my though 's inherence in a certain historical situation of its own and through that situation in other historical situations which interest i – –since it is the foundational origin and original foundation of the objective relations of which science speaks to us about – makes knowledge of the social self-knowledge, and calls forth and authorizes a view of intersubjectivity as my own which science forgets even as it utilizes it and which is proper to philosophy. Since we are hemmed in by history, it is up to us to understand that whatever truth we may have is to be gotten not despite but through our historical inherence. Superficially considered our inherence destroys all truth; considered radically, it founds a new idea of truth (1964, p. 109).

Merleau-Ponty (1964) goes on to suggest that we need to reject the idea of the spectator who has no point of view and that we truth arises in a situation in which we are involved. Rather than concluding we should not make assertions or claims, I see this as suggesting that we be open to new understandings. For example, I am confident, based on extensive research, that forgiving another involves coming to see the perpetrator as more than a victimizer and as a fellow human being (Halling, 2008). Accordingly I would rephrase the last sentence, 'There is a painful realization that we may be getting it wrong most of time,' to "we should be aware that we *might well* get It wrong, while also recognizing that the truths we arrive at, however systematically and carefully, are subject to revision and even, in some cases, subject to being overthrown. This rephrasing, I would claim, is consistent with the basic position Merleau-Ponty takes in The *Phenomenology of Perception* (1962).

Reading and reflecting on these articles has been stimulating and challenging. I have found that the most productive dialogues take place when there is a mixture of agreement and disagreement allowing for a clarification of one's own understanding and point of view as one takes into account and struggles with perspectives that that one had not previously encountered.

Disclosure statement

No potential conflict of interest was reported by the author(s).

References

Adame, A. L., Bassman, R., Morsey, M., & Yates, K. (2017). *Exploring identities of psychiatric survivor therapists: Beyond us and them*. Palgrave MacMillan.

Boisen, A. (1960). *Out of the depths: An autobiographical study of mental disorders and religious experience*. Harper.

Elliott, E., Fischer, C. T., & Rennie, D. L. (1999). Evolving guidelines for publication of qualitative research in psychology and related fields. *British Journal of Clinical Psychology*, 38(3), 215–229. https://doi.org/10.1348/014466599162782

Fischer, C. T. (1994). *Individualizing psychological assessment*. Lawrence Earlbaum.

Gadamer, H. G. (1988). *Truth and method*. New York, NY: Crossroads.

Giorgi, A. (2009). *The descriptive phenomenological method in psychology: A modified Husserlian approach*. Duquesne University Press.

Gnaulati, E. (2018). *Saving talk therapy: How health insurers, big pharma, and slanted science are running good mental health care*. Beacon Press.

Halling, S. (2002). Making phenomenology accessible to a wider audience. *Journal of Phenomenological Psychology, 33*(1), 19-38. https://doi.org/10.1163/156916202320900400

Halling, S. (2008). *Intimacy, transcendence and psychology: Closeness and openness in everyday life.* New York, NY: Palgrave Macmillan.

Halling, S. (2014). The phenomenon as muse: On being open to "friendly invasion". *Indo-Pacific Journal of Phenomenology, 14*(1), 1-10. https://doi.org/10.2989/IPJP.2014.14.1.5.1237

Halling, S., MacNabb, M., & Rowe, J. O. (2006a). Existential-phenomenological psychotherapy in the trenches: a collaborative approach to serving the underserved. *Journal of Phenomenological Psychology, 37*(2), 171-196. https://doi.org/10.1163/15691206778876335

Halling, S., Leifer, M., & Rowe, J. O. (2006b). The emergence of the dialogal approach: Forgiving another. In C. T. Fischer (Ed.), *Qualitative research for psychologists: Introduction through empirical studies* (pp. 173-212). New York, NY: Academic Press.

Heinrich, M. (2020). *Reflections of a cynical clinical psychologist.* Routledge.

Howell, P. (2000). *From a storm to w whisper.* Ulyssian.

Lawner, P. (1981). Reflections on the 'unknown' in psychotherapy. *Psychotherapy: Theory, Research and Practice, 18*(3), 306-312. https://doi.org/10.1037/h0088378

Merleau-Ponty, M. (1962). *The phenomenology of perception.* New York, NY: Humanities Press.

Merleau-Ponty, M. (1964). The philosopher and sociology. In *Signs* (pp. 98-113). Evanston, IL: Northwestern University Press.

Norris, K. (1998). *Amazing grace: A vocabulary of faith.* Penguin.

Smith, J. A., Flowers, P., & Larkin, M. (2009). *Interpretative phenomenological analysis: Theory, method, research.* SAGE.

Toback, S, Halling, S, Halverson, J. D, Loerch, D. M, McNabb, M, & Reisberg, J. (2018). Executives' experiences of envy in the workplace: a collaborative phenomenological study. *The Humanistic Psychologist, 46*(4), 361-389. doi:10.1037/hum0000094

Van Manen, M. (1997). *Researching lived experience: Human science for an action sensitive pedagogy.* Routledge.

Van Manen, M. (2017). Phenomenology in its original sense. *Qualitative Health Research, 27*(6), 810-825. https://doi.org/10.1177/1049732317699381

On the very idea of post-existentialism

Del Loewenthal

Post-existentialism was my attempt to consider the implications for therapeutic practice of the writings of such existentialists as Kierkegaard and Heidegger – without being caught up in what had seemed to become existentialism's inferred narcissism – and to reopen the question of politics and ideology in our practice. There is also here an effort to re-privilege Merleau-Ponty's phenomenology in attempting to always start with what emerges between client and practitioner, rather than to start with specific theories. Finally, it is an attempt to provide a space in which structural linguistics and various post-modern writers can be considered as having possible implications for our practice.

I am proposing a place for exploring the psychological therapies at the start of the twenty-first century that is in contrast to the prevailing culture that has led to the increasing dominance of approaches such as Cognitive Behavioural Therapy (CBT). An attempt is made to offer a space where we might still be able to think about how alienated we are through valuing existential notions such as experience and meaning, whilst questioning other aspects such as existentialism's inferred narcissism and the place it has come to take up with regards to such aspects as psychoanalysis and the political. The post-existential would also include the post-phenomenological, where, for example, Merleau-Ponty's notion of being open to what emerges in the between (Merleau-Ponty, 1962) (as well as his notion of embodiment) would be given primacy over Husserlian notions of intentionality. As a result, questions such as those of mystery, an unknown, an unconscious and the non-intentional can be re-examined. A third element to be explored will be the extent to which we might consider more recent ideas – for example, those of Saussure, Levinas, Derrida, Foucault, Lacan and Wittgenstein (as explored, for example, in Loewenthal and Snell, 2003) – without becoming too caught up in them. It is hoped that having a possible space to explore what some would now call our 'wellbeing', theoretically through post-existentialism and methodologically through post-phenomenology, can provide a loose base, with concerns of any further generalisation, for a greater possibility of accepting rather than escaping who we are.

In developing one way of starting with practice, this raises fundamental questions about the nature of knowledge in the psychological therapies and the implications for what might be meant by theory, research and indeed practice. Here, the case will be put for post-existentialism, which is in contrast to the work on existential psychotherapy as developed by Yalom (1980, 1989) in North America and Van Deurzen (1997, 2005) and Spinelli (2005) in the UK.

Why post-existentialism?

The name 'post-existentialism' is tentatively being put forward in an attempt to describe a potential cultural moment whereby the psychological therapies can at least start with practice. To give such a name, albeit to a particular loose mixture of cultural influences, is done with much trepidation and is not meant to name yet another school. However, such a branding is with some reluctance, presented as it is considered necessary to counter the hegemony of training technicians as psychological therapists (a term used here to include counsellor, psychotherapist, psychoanalyst, psychologist, art and play therapist) to oil the wheel of our increasingly dominant managerialist culture. This account expresses one way of starting with practice and then considers the implications, rather than the applications, of theory. A position is taken, more akin to Wittgenstein's, that theory as such cannot provide a foundation for the psychological therapies (Heaton, 2010). In giving a primacy to practice, various notions of phenomenology come closer to this, which most psychological therapists would associate with existentialism, though most contemporary readings of existentialism are considered dated – hence the name post-existentialism.

Whilst starting with practice (and hopefully continually attempting to return to it) is associated with ordinary language, both this and how we consider it is already mediated by the language of our contemporary culture. In working therapeutically, the psychological therapist may find that certain ideas/theories come to mind when working with a client/patient. This is regarded as very different to starting with such theories as a frame-up. I attempt to explore how various authors can hopefully enable a thoughtful return to practice. As mentioned, the term 'phenomenology' could be considered to come closest to what is being considered here. However, there have been attempts to discredit phenomenology from Foucault and others, which has led to less prominence of this term in more recent cultural developments. Though it is argued here that practice is always the basis of our work, it will always be problematic to describe this through words such as 'phenomenology' and 'tacit knowledge' – another attempt to conceptualise the essence of practice. It is also argued that by linking phenomenology with developments in structural linguistics, it is possible to consider the political in terms of chains of signifiers. It would also appear that phenomenologists, alongside most psychological therapists, do not seem adept at political consideration outside their immediate training institute. There is a further suggestion that we consider the term 'post-phenomenological' to free us of some of phenomenology's previous connotations whilst continuing with, for example, the notion of what emerges in the between (Merleau-Ponty, 1962). It is recognised that, in construing the names post-existentialism and post-phenomenology, this is not ordinary language and that attempting to put the case of using these terms to stay with practice and ordinary language is at best a paradox. It is however hoped that if post-existentialism is considered as a temporary device, then the benefits in attempting to return to at least starting with practice will outweigh the hypocrisy.

Following Laing (1960) and others, I have previously used the term 'existential–analytic' to describe a practice, which might have been seen to originate from Pyrrhonian scepticism. However, 'existentialism' seems increasingly stuck in its self-centredness and 'analytic' appears to increasingly imply a frame-up whereby psychological therapists are meant to be able to diagnose and treat patients in terms of an unconscious as if they were modern medical doctors. Existentialism was therefore losing its original meaning of being 'astonishing' and analysis was appearing less a practice of thoughtfulness and more the reverse, through the application of technologies. Something else therefore appears needed so that one can explore what emerges in practice between psychological therapist and patient/client.

We appear to be in a managerial culture where CBT is the therapy of choice. CBT has numerous variants but its fundamental assumption is to change the way we think from where we find ourselves. This taking our minds off what comes to us can be useful, but as has been argued elsewhere (Loewenthal and House, 2010, House and Loewenthal, 2007) is disastrous as an overall approach for a culture, as it means we can never come to our senses. What if we want to allow thoughts to come to us? There are arguments that we are unable to allow such thoughts either because of, for example, existential anxieties such as death or psychoanalytic anxieties as signified by the oedipal complex. So how could one be with a psychological therapist who, rather than lead us to stop thinking, might enable us to work through that which blocks our thinking so we can breathe more easily? Such a practice – which might include what Kierkegaard (1944) has described as education through 'dread' (where one might find it hard to breathe, in order to eventually breathe more easily) – could start with meaning, but in contrast to CBT might be more influenced by Heidegger's notions of being in the world with others (Heidegger, 1927). Yet how could one consider such a space in contrast to CBT, which would potentially allow for other developments in our cultural practice such as structural linguistics and post-modernism?

Post-modernism can be seen to consider the person not as a 'subject' but as decentred and 'subject to' (Loewenthal and Snell, 2003). One important example of this is that, following the work of Saussure (1959), we are subject to language – an example of cultural development of potential interest to anyone interested in a talking cure! Another currently important figure is Levinas as he suggests that if we are to consider our being, then we need to try and start not with such self-centredness that sets up the world so that everything returns to me but instead be strong enough to first consider our responsibility for others (Levinas, 1961). Such thinking may have the potential for us then to think of meaning without excluding questions of an unconscious, but in a way that counters the consumerist managerialist forces in our society (Loewenthal, 2010), which are relentlessly destroying our communities, particularly for our children (House and Loewenthal, 2010) and ourselves.

Post-existentialism is therefore an attempt for us to experience our alienation in the hope that we may still be able, individually and collectively, to do more about it. Further, it is an attempt to consider a potential cultural practice which, in contrast to what is taken as CBT, considers psychological therapy as essentially subversive: personally in not excluding thoughts and politically in terms of our relationship with others.

'Post-post-modernism' is another term that could have been used. Post-modernism is considered to have made important contributions in opening up possibilities for the psychological therapies, yet to stay with it might mean we would be unable to communicate with anyone. Post-existentialism is therefore in some ways a return to Heidegger's questions of being-in-the-world-with-others, exploring such meanings in their specific context without ignoring the work of the post-modernists, psychoanalysts or the political.

Therefore, it is hoped we may identify a way of challenging a dominant discourse by revitalising previous approaches by, in some way, going back to where we are coming from. In this sense, as Lyotard (1979) points out, the word post does not only mean after. ...

Finally, there is yet another response to the question 'why post-existentialism?' The first time I gave a talk on this subject at an international conference was when I was invited to speak at the American Psychological Association annual conference in Hawaii in 2004 and present a paper called 'Post-phenomenology.' Afterwards, as I was leaving the lecture theatre, a member of the audience who I had not yet met tugged at my sleeve and said, 'You know, we would understand it much better if you called it "post-existentialism".' Hope you do!

What is post-existentialism?

This account of post-existentialism describes work in progress at the Centre for Therapeutic Education, Roehampton University, UK (where we carry out research and train counsellors, psychotherapists and psychologists). We are all practitioners (psychological therapists) with a particular interest in the implications of continental philosophy for practice, which I have termed 'post-existential'. As has been said, this development is in contrast to the rapid growth of Cognitive Behavioural Therapy in what some would term our current 'age of happiness' (Layard 2006, Seligman, 1995). CBT can be seen to include a way of not thinking, which can be useful at times but catastrophic as the main approach to wellbeing. The post-existential takes as an important influence Heidegger's *dasein* in exploring the 'well' in terms of 'being' (in the world with others), and is a particular mixture of some aspects of existentialism, phenomenology and post-modernism.

'Post-existential' is taken to mean 'after' Heidegger (1962) and – in a different way – after Husserl's phenomenology (1983), yet looking to retain what might be good from existentialism together with aspects of subsequent developments such as post-modernism. At the very least we might consider, as David Cooper suggests, that existentialism 'is worth revisiting at intervals for the help it may offer with themes of contemporary interest' (Cooper, 1990: vii).

So let's start by briefly going back to what might have been meant by existentialism – a name probably originating from Gabriel Marcel (Cooper 2003) and then taken up, at first very reluctantly, by other French philosophers such as Jean-Paul Sartre (1943) and Simone de Beauvoir (1972), though perhaps becoming particularly grounded in Martin Heidegger's work on existence, which he in turn developed from the work of Kierkegaard (1941, 1980) and Nietzsche (1883, 1974) and, particularly with regard to phenomenology, Husserl (1983).

Whilst there appears to be no agreed definition, David Cooper provides a parody of what was taken as existence: '... a constant *striving*, a perpetual *choice*: it is marked by a radical *freedom*, and *responsibility*. And it is also prey to a sense of *Angst* which reveals that, for the most part, it is lived *inauthentically* and in *bad faith*. And because the character of the human life is never *given*, existence is *without foundation*; hence it is *abandoned* or *absurd* even' (Cooper, 1990: 3–4). However, how one responds to these existential concerns is vital in a way, whilst there is no agreement as to what existentialism 'is'. For many in the 1950s and 60s, the method of existentialism was phenomenology, which was particularly developed by Heidegger's teacher Edmund Husserl through the encouragement of Wilhelm Wundt, regarded by many as a founding father of psychology. Whilst

Wilhelm Wundt was one of those who persuaded Husserl away from his more quantitative interests to develop Brentano's (1995a) descriptive psychology (whose audience included not only Husserl but one Sigmund Freud), Wundt (1904) considered psychology to be partly a natural science and partly a social science.

Hence, if we return to David Cooper's parody of existential terms, and if we attempt to study them experimentally, this could be very different to a study that looks at what emerges in terms of meanings. Thus, for Brentano (1995b) experimentalism is not appropriate, whereas current psychological practice has increasingly been dismissive of phenomenology. Husserl's hope for a pure phenomenology which we do not contaminate was not considered to be possible by the likes of Heidegger, Merleau-Ponty or Sartre. Nevertheless, Heidegger managed to marry existentialism and phenomenology and Merleau-Ponty developed a notion of meaning emerging in the between, which became more dominant until Foucault (1974) and others questioned whether phenomenology was still relevant after the advent of structuralism and the developing influence of Saussure and structural linguistics. Later, Derrida (1990) importantly questioned if any system of thought – whether, for example, phenomenology, structuralism or psychoanalysis – would always be blinded by its own definition. Yet would it not be possible to look at some questions regarding our being existentially – without this being about nostalgia (Oakley 1990) or an attempt to return to something that probably never existed (Borsch-Jacobsen 1991)?

The versions of existentialism that appeared in the English-speaking world seemed to remove such issues of politics and psychoanalysis – unlike, for example, Continental Europe, where Sartre would come to explore existentialism and Marxism and Binswanger would speak of the existential analyst who 'not only is in possession of existential–analytic and psychotherapeutic competence, but ... he must dare to risk committing his own existence in the struggle for the freedom of his partners' (Binswanger in Friedman 1991: 426). Binswanger, of course, later said he had misunderstood Heidegger's notion of being, though he did say he felt it was a fruitful misunderstanding! Heidegger, in turn, considered Sartre's understanding of his (Heidegger's) work as rubbish. Heidegger did work with Medard Boss, who some felt therefore had the nearest possibility of looking at the implications of Heidegger's writings for existential practice. Interestingly, the so-called 'British school' of existentialism adopted more of Boss's work but attempted to drop Boss's interest in and strong influence from psychoanalysis (Cooper, 2003). This is again in contrast to those who start with psychoanalysis and then consider the existential–phenomenological (Askay and Farquhar 2006). Neither are what is termed here the 'post-existential'.

We thus have the most popular currents of existential psychotherapy in the UK (as represented by Van Deurzen, 1997 and Spinelli, 2007) and in North America (as represented by May, 1996 and Yalom, 1980) presented as not requiring the possession of existential analytic competence as essential and removing, in general, the political. The existential movement has a history of aristocratic and indeed what are sometimes seen as Fascist political tendencies. Yet, couldn't post-existentialism combine, for example, Foucauldian notions of power with existential concerns and couldn't post-existential practice explore the unknown, including an unconscious? Not wishing to start with psychoanalytic theories seems very different to allowing them to sometimes come to mind. Thus, one fundamental difference between the post-existentialist, and particularly Anglo-Saxonised, existentialism is the former's acknowledgement that inevitably we are all subject-to. So the rejection of psychoanalytic dogma as a starting model does not mean, or indeed is a rationalisation for, an attempt to be subject-to nothing.

It is here where the post-modern (Loewenthal and Snell 2003) may bring about the greatest change to what was regarded as existentialism in that we are seen as being, for example, subject-to language (Lacan), writing (Derrida), ethics (Levinas) and an unconscious (Freud). Thus, Sartre's 'I am my choices' could be regarded as representing a very narcissistic age. In contrast the post-existential person would be regarded as only having some agency with an attempt towards a responsibility. For example, it might be that in growing up someone took a survival path, which may have been necessary then but may now be redundant and unhelpful to this person or others – perhaps he was therefore less able to take responsibility for who he was then but has more, but not complete, agency as to where he finds himself now. Furthermore, whilst aspects of learning theory may be of help here, though more likely in the context of Polyani's (1983) tacit knowledge, we might also be able to see constrictions in ourselves and how we constrict others politically – with both sizes of the letter 'p' – as well as how our intentions are not always clear to us.

Foucault became interested in power and knowledge and the political status of psychiatry as science. With post-existentialism we would now, in exploring our wellbeing, raise questions of power, knowledge and the political nature of psychology as science. This would in some ways be similar to how Foucault and some existentialists questioned the political status of psychiatry as science, and at least a primacy would be given to first thinking of what is termed 'mental illness' as dissimilar to a physical illness but instead more to do with relations with others. Yet there would be vitally important distinctions: Foucault (1974) abandoned his early interest in phenomenology. But was this, as Hoeller (1986) points out, because he took Husserl's notion of transcendental phenomenology, which does not really allow for the historical and cultural? As further argued by Hoeller (1986), Heidegger, with his *dasein* as being in the historical/cultural world with others, enables phenomenology to be released from Husserl's attempts to show a pure subjectivity and thus 'a universal doctrine of the structures of individual subjectivity and intersubjectivity' (Husserl 1977: 178–179). This opening up of phenomenology was further developed for psychotherapy by Binswanger, Boss and Laing, and we term this 'post-phenomenology' to distinguish it from Husserl's original transcendental phenomenology. Thus if we could both be attentive to what emerges in the between of client and therapist and be aware of what is regarded culturally and historically as common sense we could have an interest in how our clients and those around them have brought and bring pressures on each other. This meeting, which could include the implications for the present of the client's history and the history of the culture, without being caught up in a potentially totalising approach (in this case, for example, Foulcaudian genealogy), would be an example of post-phenomenology. It might also be closer to what those such as Wilheim Wundt saw as psychology, though the post-existential should, it is suggested, always be beyond.

One exception to those existentialists mentioned earlier, and who may be regarded as leading to post-existentialism, is R.D. Laing (1990, 1969). He, as with existentialism, was able to keep something open without defining it in a positivistic way, removing the danger that can happen through taking away the mystery of taking away the thing itself (Merleau-Ponty 1962). Laing, for example, suggested that whilst behaviour is important, what is really important is how one experiences behaviour (Laing 1967). Here again, Laing and those influenced by him are not being put forward as if their approach is the ideal, but they are able to hold a space which is always only partially defined and where something helpful for our thoughtfulness may at times emerge.

One result of all this concerns what we regard as psychology. For those such as Binswanger, who might be seen in some ways to be more in keeping with Wundt:

> When this *my*, or *our*, this *I* or *he* or *we* are bracketed out, the result is that psychology becomes ;impersonal' and 'objective' while losing, at the same time, the scientific character of a genuine psychologist and becoming, instead, natural science ... In place of a reciprocal, 'personal' communication within a we-relationship we find a one-sided, i.e., irreversible, relationship between doctor and patient and an even more impersonal relationship between researcher and the object of research. Experience, participation and confrontation between human beings in the present moment gives way to the 'perfect tense' of theoretical investigation.
>
> (Binswanger in Friedman 1991: 414)

Thus unfortunately, 'good' psychological research is currently determined by publication in quantitative, primarily American, journals and relations between people are more for English departments, where there is usually more chance of studying not only Freud and Lacan but Derrida, Foucault et al. In the social sciences, there is a historical, cultural shift to behaviouralism, with desperate concerns for survival by some to quantify experience to show that it is evidence-based. Yet, what is denied keeps re-emerging and questions have again recently been raised as to whether psychology should really be the science of experience rather than the science of the mind (Ashworth, 2004).

So post-existentialism can be seen to be attempting to find a place between existentialism and post-post-modernism, enabling us to take from the existential and the post-modern that which can be helpful to us in exploring our existence at the start of the twenty-first century. Another dimension of post-existentialism is to find a place between natural and social science, for starting with notions of existence is to imply starting with the human soul (Plato, in Cushman, 2001) and the historical and cultural aspects of social (rather than starting with the natural) science. With this emerge the possibilities of a political viewpoint, which could engage with various notions of, for example, democracy and the notion of an unconscious coming more from those such as Kierkegaard (1941, 1980) and Nietzsche (1883, 1974). Such possibilities open up returning psychology to its philosophical roots and with it, important implications for those practices aimed at promoting wellbeing – including the way we train our students.

I have previously attempted to explore some of these dimensions: initially through how individuals and structures in society conspire to produce a form of alienating escape motivation (Loewenthal, 2002). More recently I have been interested in exploring, on the one hand, how post-modernism has emerged from phenomenology (Loewenthal and Snell, 2003) and on the other, evaluating the usefulness of qualitative research for exploring relational aspects in therapy, with particular reference to the post-existential (Loewenthal 2007).

References

Ashworth, P. (2004). The origins of qualitative psychology. In J. A. Smith (Ed.) *Qualitative Psychology: A Practical Guide to Research Methods*. London: Sage (pp. 4–24).

Askay, R. and Farquhar, J. (2006). *Apprehending the Inaccessible: Freudian Psychoanalysis and Existential Phenomenology*. Evanston, Il: Northwestern University Press.

Binswanger, L. (1991) in Friedman, M., *The Worlds of Existentialism: A Critical Reader*. New York: Delmar Publishers, (pp. 414–426).
Borch-Jacobsen, M. (1991). *Lacan: The Absolute Master*. Stanford, CA: Stanford University Press.
Brentano, F. (1995a). *Descriptive Psychology*. London: Routledge.
Brentano, F. (1995b[1874]). *Psychology from an Empirical Standpoint*. London: Routledge.
Cooper, M. (2003). *Existential Therapies*. London: Routledge.
Cooper, D. E. (1990). *Existentialism: A Reconstruction*. Oxford: Blackwell Publishing.
Cushman, R. (2001). *Therapeia: Plato's Conception of Philosophy*. New Jersey: Transaction Publishers.
De Beauvoir, S. (1972[1949]). *The Second Sex* (H. M. Parshley, Trans.) London: Penguin.
Derrida J. (1990). *Resistances to Psychoanalysis*. Stanford: Stanford University Press.
Foucault, M. (1974[1954]). *The Psychological Dimensions of Mental Illness* (A. M. Sheridan-Smith, Trans.). New York: Harper and Row.
Heaton, J. M. (2010). *The Talking Cure: Wittgenstein's Therapeutic Method for Psychotherapy*. London: Palgrave Macmillan.
Heidegger, M. (1962[1927]). *Being and Time* (J. Macquarrie and E. S. Robinson, Trans.). London: Harper and Row.
Hoeller, K. (1986). Editor's foreword: dream and existence. *Special Issue of Review of Existential Psychology and Psychiatry*, 7–17.
Husserl, E. (1977). *Phenomenological Psychology* (J. Scanlon, Trans.). Nijhoff: The Hague.
Husserl, E. (1983). *Ideas Pertaining to a Pure Phenomenology and to a Phenomenological Philosophy* (F. Kersten, Trans.). Nijhoff: The Hague.
Kierkegaard, S. (1980[1844]). *The Concept of Anxiety* (R. Thomte, Trans.). Princeton: Princeton University Press.
Kierkegaard, S. (1941[1855]). *The Sickness unto Death* (W. Lowrie, Trans.). Princeton: Princeton University Press.
Kierkegaard, S. (1944[1848]). The concept of dread (W. Lowry, Trans.). In Friedman, M. (Ed.) (1964). *The Worlds of Existentialism: A Critical Reader*. New York: Random House (pp. 369–371).
Laing, R. D. (1990[1960]). *The Divided Self: An Existential Study in Sanity and Madness*. Harmondsworth: Penguin.
Laing, R. D. (1967). *The Politics of Experience*. London: Tavistock Publications.
Laing, R. D. (1969). *Self and Others* (second edition). London: Routledge.
Layard, R. (2006). *Happiness: Lessons from a New Science*. London: Penguin.
Levinas, E. (1961). *Totality and Infinity: An Essay on Exteriority* (A. Lingis, Trans.). Pittsburgh: Duquesne University Press.
Loewenthal, D. (2002). Involvement and Emotional Labour. *Soundings*, 20: 151–162.
Loewenthal, D. (2007). Relational research, ideology and the evolution of intersubjectivity in a post-existential culture. In D. Loewenthal (Ed.), *Case Studies in Relational Research*. London: Palgrave Macmillan (pp. 221–240).
Loewenthal, D. (2011). On the very idea of post-existentialism. In D. Loewenthal, *Post-Existentialism and the Psychological Therapies: Towards a Therapy without Foundations*, London: Karnac (pp. 1–12).
Loewenthal, D. and Snell, R. (2003). *Post-Modernism for Psychotherapists*. London: Routledge.
Loewenthal, D. and House, R. (Eds.) (2010). *Critically Engaging CBT*. Maidenhead: Open University Press.
Lyotard, J-F. (1979). *The Postmodern Condition: A Report on Knowledge*. Minneapolis: University of Minnesota Press.
May, R. (1996[1950]). *The Meaning of Anxiety* (revised edition). New York: W. W. Norton.
Merleau-Ponty, M. (1962). *The Phenomenology of Perception* (C. Smith, Trans.). London: Routledge Kegan-Paul.
Nietzsche, F. (1933[1883]). *Thus spoke Zarathustra*, (A. Tille, Trans.). New York: Dutton.
Nietzsche, F. (1974[1888]). *The Gay Science* (W. Kaufman, Trans.). New York: Vintage Books.
Oakley, C. (1990). An account of the first conference of the society for existential analysis. *Journal of Existential Analysis*, 1(1): 38–45.

Polyani, M. (1983[1966]). *The Tacit Dimension*. Gloucester, MA: Peter Smith.

Saussure, F. de. (1959). *Course in General Linguistics*. London: Fontana.

Sartre, J. P. (1943[1956]). *Being and Nothingness: An Essay on Phenomenological Ontology* (H. Barnes, Trans.). New York: Philosophical Library.

Seligman, M. (1995). The effectiveness of psychotherapy: the consumer reports study. *American Psychologist*, 50(12): 965–974.

Spinelli, E. (2005). *The Interpreted World: An Introduction toPphenomenological Psychology* (second edition). London: Sage.

Spinelli, E. (2007). *Practicing Existential Psychotherapy: The Relational World*. London: Sage.

Van Deurzen, E. (1997). *Everyday Mysteries: Existential Dimensions of Psychotherapy*. London: Routledge.

Van Deurzen, E. and Kenward, R. (2005). *Dictionary of Existential Psychotherapy and Counselling*. London: Sage.

Wundt, W. (1904[1874]). *Principles of Physiological Psychology* (E. B. Tichener, Trans.). London: Allen.

Yalom, R. (1980). *Existential Psychotherapy*. New York: Basic Books.

Yalom, I. D. (1989). *Love's Executioner, and Other Tales of Psychotherapy*. New York: Harper Perennial.

Index

Abgehobenheit 113
Adorno, T. 106
Altson, Catherine 6, 113
Amazing Grace (Norris) 136–7
'American dream' 106
'The Analytical Situation as a Dynamic Field' 127n2
Andén, L. 33
anti-psychiatry 12
Armstrong, N. 60
authenticity 60, 80, 84, 104–5, 113
Avdi, Evrinomy 5

Bachelard, G. 38, 136
Badiou, A. 126
Balint, Michael 24
Baranger, Willy 119, 127n2
Barrett, William 138
Bazzano, Manu 7
Beecrof, Gauri 6
Benjamin, Jessica 120
Bertrand, Betty 6, 113
blind recognition 36, 37
'bloody foreigners' 15–16
Boisen, Anton 134
Bracken, P. 12, 16
Braun, V. 90
Brentano, F. 147
Britain 12, 15
'British school' of existentialism 147
Brooks, Onel 6
Buckland, Christian 6

catatonic schizophrenia 137
Cayne, Julia 6, 107, 110–11, 120, 124
Chernaik, Laura 7
'civilised people' 22–3
Clarke, V. 90
co-constituting intersubjectivity 53
Cognitive Behavioural Therapy (CBT) 143, 145–6

Comans, K. 60
compassion fatigue 92
compliance 15, 104–5, 118, 134
composite depiction 93, 95–7
'compromising land' 15
conformity 13, 15, 104–5, 109, 118, 134
conquistador 13, 22, 105
continuous professional development (CPD) courses 1, 3
controversial discussions 12
Cooper, David 146–7
counter-tradition 113
countertransference 123–6, 127n2
creative synthesis 62, 65, 94–5, 98–100
critical existential-analytic psychotherapies 131
critical psychiatry 12

de Beauvoir, Simone 146
Derrida, J. 3, 12, 143, 147, 149
Descriptive Phenomenological Approach (DPA) 79, 85, 132
Descriptive Phenomenological Method (DPM) 135–6, 139
Dreyfus, H. 36
Dunnes, A. 78

'ecumenical' 132
effective psychotherapy 5
Elliston, F. 52
emotional essence 34
empirical phenomenology 43, 46, 118–19, 122–3
enigmatic 125, 138
enunciation 121
epistemological foundations 119–20
essence 3, 34, 36, 46, 61, 71, 79–82, 85, 93–4, 97, 100, 108–9, 120–4, 136, 144
European 106–7
evidence-based practice 4, 7
exemplary portraits 93–4, 97–8

explication 62, 64–5
Exploring identities of psychiatric survivor therapists: Beyond us and them (Adame) 134

Fanon, F. 119
Ferenczi, Sandor 25–6
filiation 118–19, 124
Finlay, Linda 6
Fischer, C. T. 140
foreignness 6, 14, 18, 22–3, 104, 118–20, 134
Foucault, M. 143, 147–9
free imaginative variation 79
Freud, Sigmund 3, 13–14, 23, 75, 83, 105–7, 124, 127n3, 128n5, 149

Gadamer, H-G. 3, 140
Gaitanidis, Anastasios 5
Gelassenheit (letting beings be) 49
gesture 6, 107–9, 120–1, 124, 136; *see also* Merleau-Ponty, M.
Giorgi, Amedeo 37, 43, 45–6, 48, 52–3, 79, 85, 110, 118, 121, 135–7
Glover, Edward 14
Gomez, Lavina 23–4
'Great Depression' 2
Green, Andre 127n3
Greenblat, L. 60
Guba, E. 38

Halling, Steen 7
Heidegger, Martin 3–4, 43, 49, 51, 138, 146
Heinrich, Max 135
hermeneutics of suspicion 4
heterotopia 125–6
heuristic: research 59, 61, 64, 93, 114; self-search inquiry 111; *see also* self-search inquiry; sexual abuse *see* sexual abuse
Heuristic Inquiry approach 133
Heuristic Self-Search Inquiry (HSSI) 62–4
hindrance factors 96
Hoeller, K. 148
Howell, Patrick 134
humour 81, 112–13, 136; adaptive to situations 81; communication and physical expression 82; form of connection 80; form of emotion 79–80; power 80; relational 82; relaxing and comforting 82
Husserl, Edmund 4, 43–4, 46, 49, 52–3, 78, 110–11, 138, 146
'hypertrophied consciousness' 105

illumination 64–5
The Illusion of Technique (Barrett) 138
immersed 62, 64–5
incubation 62, 64
individual depictions 93–5
inferred narcissism 7, 143
initial engagement 61–2, 64
intentionality 126–7, 143
Interpretative Phenomenological Analysis (IPA) 4, 132, 137
intersectionality 22

Jones, Ernest 15

Kareem, Jaffa 12
Kearney, R. 12
Kierkegaard, S. 4, 16, 38, 104, 145–6, 149
Kristeva, J. 12
Kubie, L. 77

Lacan, J. 3, 33, 127n4, 143, 149
Laing, R. D. 12, 144, 148
la langue (structural aspects of language) 31, 34, 136
language 12, 26, 30–2, 47, 52–3, 63, 79, 85, 107–10, 136, 144–5, 148; Merleau-Ponty's phenomenology 39; and Saussure, D. F. 32–3; from structural theory to gestural phenomena 33–6
la parole (usage of language) 31, 34, 136
Laplanche, J. 125
Lave, J. 5
Lawner, Peter 134, 140
Lawrence, Sacha 6
Levinas, E. 3–4, 12, 143
liberalism 16–17
Lincoln, Y. 38
L'individuation psychique et collective (Simondon) 111
linguistics 32
Littlewood, Roland 12
Loewenthal, Del 1, 6–7, 58, 70, 110–11, 113, 131
Lothane, Z. 76
Lyotard, J-F. 104, 146

Marcus, N. 76
Marxism 16–17, 147
McCormick, P. 52
McLeod, J. 58
McSherry, Tony 6, 110–11, 121, 123–4
meaning, private life of 33–8, 82–5, 108–11, 122, 124–6; constriction of 44; empirical method, phenomenology and psychotherapeutic research 52–3; 50;

Giorgi's empirical phenomenological method 46–8; Husserl's phenomenology 50; landscapes of 51–2; mental health nursing 43–6; 'originary giving intuition' 51; phenomenological approach 48–9; psychotherapy *see* psychotherapy; 'sensual' 49–50; truthfulness 53; units 37
mediated immediacy 113
mental health nursing 43–6
mental illness 45, 58–9, 148
Merleau-Ponty, M. 4, 31–2, 34–6, 43, 49, 108, 124, 136, 138, 140; between body and method 36–9; and language 32–3; phenomenology 39–40; 'spontaneous gesture' 30; story and gesture 31–2; structural linguistics 30–1; structural theory to gestural phenomena 33–6; the Visible and the Invisible 31; 'through a glass darkly' 30
modernism 16, 26, 103–4; and universal application 16–17
modernist 16, 24, 104, 107, 145
modernity 16, 75, 119
Moustakas, C. E. 61–2, 64, 93, 118, 121–2, 124, 134

native informants 119, 122
neuro-phenomenology 112
Nicholl, Elizabeth 6, 122, 126, 133
Nietzsche, F. 4, 16, 104, 146, 149
non-intentional 39
Norris, Kathleen 136–7

Oedipus complex 17
On Narcissism (Freud) 127n3
ontology of actuality 107
originary giving intuitions 46, 48, 50–1
origins of the study 44–6, 121
Osborne, Seth 6
Out of the Depths (Boisen) 134
Oxford Dictionary Online 75

Panichelli, C. 83
Parsloe, Sally 6
'pathological' fixations 127n3
'peaceful compromising land' 15
Pearlman, L. A. 91
phenomenology 1, 3–4, 6–7, 31, 37–40, 43–4, 46, 48, 50, 52–3, 78, 108–13, 118, 123, 132, 136, 139, 144
The Phenomenology of Perception (Merleau-Ponty) 33, 36, 141
Philadelphia Association 12
Phillips, Adam 12

The Philosopher and Sociology (Merleau-Ponty) 140
philosophical anthropology 113
philosophy 12, 45, 107, 112, 120, 140, 146
Plessner, Helmut 113
"political correctness" 92
Polyani, M. 148
post-existentialism 1, 3, 143–9
postmodernism 16–17, 25–6, 103–4, 119
post-phenomenology 146
postqualitative 7, 108, 112
poststructuralism 104–5, 107, 109, 112
primacy of the other 107
primitive people 22–3
prior pre-comprehension (proto-comprehension) 111
psychoanalysis 3, 7, 11, 104, 106–7, 109, 119–20, 127n1, 134–5, 143, 147; assumptions and convictions 11; in Britain and the United States 12; client example 19–22; conquests and compromises 13–16; contemporary courses 11; definition 11, 13; foreigner 25–7; illustrations 17–19; modernism and universal application 16–17; universal application 22–5; Women's Therapy Centre in London 12
psychoanalytical theory 125
psychoanalytic perspectives 7, 75
psychotherapeutic research 5, 42–54, 58–9, 110, 118, 138
psychotherapy 1–5, 11–12, 17, 25, 60, 71, 75, 78, 105–6; challenge of 134–5; diagnosis of catatonic schizophrenia 137; DPM 135–6, 139; 'ecumenical' 132; field of mental health 135; heuristic approach 133–4; Heuristic Inquiry approach 133; humour 136; *The Illusion of Technique* 138; mental health community 134; Moustakas' method 134; pedagogical experiment 137; *Phenomenology of Perception* 141; research process 140; *Saving Talk Therapy: How Health Insurers, Big Pharma, and Slanted Science are Ruining Good Mental Health Care* 131; therapeutic interactions 138; vicarious traumatization 133; working-class background 135

qualitative research 38, 58, 70, 108, 112–13, 122, 132–3, 149

Reducing the Storm to a Whisper (Howell) 134
The researcher as psychotherapist 65, 68–9
reverie 37–9, 120
Richman, R. 76–7
Ricoeur, P. 4
Rodman, Robert 26
Rogers, C. 77
Rose, Jacqueline 106
Roustang, F. 127n4
Rutherford, K. 77

Saakvitne, K. W. 91
Said, E. W. 106
Sanderson, C. 92
Sartre, Jean-Paul 146
Sarup, M. 33
Saussure, D. F. 32–4, 136, 143, 145
savage creatures 52
Saving Talk Therapy: How Health Insurers, Big Pharma, and Slanted Science are Ruining Good Mental Health Care (Gnaulati) 131
Scheler, Max 113
schizophrenia 58–60, 65–9, 89, 111, 118, 122–3, 133, 137
Schmidt, J. 33
scientism 111
Scott-Rosales, Laura 5
'screeching wild birds' 51, 109–11
secondary traumatic stress 92
secondary traumatisation 92
Second Commandment 27
Sela-Smith, S. 61–4, 69–71, 118, 121–2, 124
self-alienation 51–2
self-search inquiry 118, 122, 133; bracketing or epoche 70; heuristic research 59, 64–9; individuals' experiences of illness 58; literature 59–60; Moustakas' heuristic inquiry 61–2; from Moustakas to Sela-Smith 62–4; 'schizophrenia' experience 58–9; scientific and technical thinking 58; Sela-Smith, S. 69–71
Sen, D. 60
sense of unconscious and conscious 121–2
sensual context 46–7
sensual meaning 49
sexual abuse 114, 133; academic literature 99; composite depiction 95–7; creative synthesis 98–9; data processing 93–4; definitions 90; exemplary portraits 97–8; gender issues 92; heuristic inquiry 92–3; in-depth exploration of therapists' experiences 100; individual depictions 94–5; interviews 93; limitations 100; participants 93; personal experiences and self-awareness 90; personal exploration of therapists' experiences 99–100; professional issues 91–2; stages of research process 89–90; therapists' responses to clients' disclosure 91; traumatic impact on therapists working 92
sexuality 23
Simondon, Gilbert 111
Smith, Jonathan 137
socio-political context 11
Spinelli, E. 144
The Splitting of the Ego in the Process of Defence (Freud) 127n3
spontaneous gesture 32
Stern, H. W. 32, 136
Stimmung 109
Strachey, James 14–15
Sultanoff, S. M. 77
superiority theory 75

Talens, Patricia 6, 112
'the body' 32–6, 39, 109
therapeutic process 58, 76, 82, 91, 93, 95–6, 100–1
'things themselves' 110
Thomas, P. 12, 16
Toback, S. 139
training institution 123
transcendental homelessness 106
Trichkova, Iana 6, 113–14, 123–4
truthfulness 6, 43–5, 49–53

'unconscious' 75–6
United States, the 12, 132, 135
'universally applicable' 24–6, 134

Vaillant, G. E. 76
Valle, R. 78
Van Deurzen, E. 144
van Kaam, A. 53
Van Manen, M. 139
vectoralism 104
vicarious traumatization 92, 133
'The Visible and Invisible' (1968) 31, 33–4

Watts, Jay 5
Welton, D. 52
Wenger, E. 5
Willig, C. 92

Winnicott, Donald 24, 26, 30–2, 77–8, 108, 120, 136
Winter, David 5, 58
Wittgenstein, L. 16, 24–5, 44, 49, 53, 104, 118, 143–4
Women's Therapy Centre in London 12
The Work of the Negative (Green) 127n3
Wundt, Wilhelm 146–7

Yalom, I. D. 144
Yalom, R. 144

youth service: anxiety 84; communication of multi-layered meanings 83; counselling service 84; discomfort 84; DPA 85; feelings of intimacy and unity 84; 'free imaginative variation' 79; Giorgi, A. 79; humour 74; *see also* humour; literature review 75–8; physical movement 85; professional role 83; sexual experiences 84; therapists 75, 83; time 78; unreflective and habitual science 78